LEE

IN THE
LOWCOUNTRY

LEE
IN THE
LOWCOUNTRY

DEFENDING CHARLESTON & SAVANNAH
1861–1862

DANIEL J. CROOKS JR.
SERIES EDITOR DOUGLAS W. BOSTICK

THE
History
PRESS

Published by The History Press
Charleston, SC 29403
www.historypress.net

Copyright © 2008 by Daniel J. Crooks Jr.
All rights reserved

Front cover: *Guns of Autumn* by Mort Künstler ©2000 Mort Künstler, Inc.
Back cover: Lee as he appeared in early 1861. *Courtesy of Douglas W. Bostick.*

Cover design by Marshall Hudson

First published 2008
Second printing 2010

Manufactured in the United States

ISBN 978.1.59629.589.6

Library of Congress Cataloging-in-Publication Data

Crooks, Daniel J.
Lee in the lowcountry : defending Charleston & Savannah, 1861-1862 / Daniel J.
Crooks, Jr.
p. cm.
Includes bibliographical references.
ISBN 978-1-59629-589-6
1. Lee, Robert E. (Robert Edward), 1807-1870--Military leadership. 2. Command of
troops--Case studies. 3. Confederate States of America. Army--History. 4. Confederate
States of America--Defenses--History. 5. Generals--Confederate States of America--
Biography. 6. United States--History--Civil War, 1861-1865--Campaigns. 7. Atlantic
Coast (S.C.)--History, Military--19th century. 8. Atlantic Coast (Ga.)--History, Military-
-19th century. 9. Charleston Region (S.C.)--History, Military--19th century. 10.
Savannah Region (Ga.)--History, Mililtary--19th century. I. Title.
E467.1.L4C85 2008
973.7'31--dc22
2008041956

For my two bookends: Daniel and Leah.

Contents

Preface

The commemoration of the 150th anniversary of the American Civil War is upon us. Unlike the centennial events that recalled the "Yanks whipping the Rebels," the current emphasis is on understanding the war and its consequences, a goal both complex and elusive.

Being from Charleston, I admit my bias in suggesting that the reader begin any such study in the city where the whole debacle began. Center of the vilified slave trade, site of the Secession Convention of 1860 and home to Fort Sumter and other coastal fortifications, Charleston is a city where the nineteenth century gently coexists with the twenty-first.

The Charleston Museum and the Old Slave Mart offer excellent interpretations of cotton production and slave barter. Numerous grand house museums beckon the traveler to enter into the world of yesteryear, with mahogany dining tables replete with the finest sterling and china. Nearby, plantations present dramatic programs on life in the era of "king cotton."

In the heart of downtown Charleston stands the Confederate Museum. Operated by the Charleston chapter of the United Daughters of the Confederacy since 1894, its collection of relics is incredible. Here, the story of Charleston and its formation as an independent commonwealth is told in terms of heroism and patriotism to a cause lost on the field of battle.

Let Charleston be your first of many new adventures in rediscovering the story of a nation torn apart. I look forward to seeing you soon as the moss-draped oaks shade your stroll through the city forever known as "the cradle of secession."

Introduction

The historian Bruce Catton once said of Robert E. Lee's early career: "If he had disappeared from view at the end of 1861, he would figure in today's footnotes as a promising officer, who somehow did not live up to expectations." In 1861, Lee was a man rooted in reality. All around him, Lee saw the lack of resources needed to make war. Far from conceding a contest that was ordained to fail, Lee forged ahead with a resolve to get Virginia and the Confederacy ready to meet the Federal onslaught. Lee oversaw the recruits as they were mustered, equipped and drilled. The Rebel army that fought at Bull Run was the product of organizational genius.

Confederate President Jefferson Davis sent his general to western Virginia in the fall of 1861 to break a stalemate between two generals who were more focused on their own personal differences than on the enemy army that was approaching. Their commanding officer was unable, or unwilling, to bring the men to a compromise. Davis knew Lee's personality well and was confident in his unassuming ways. Though the task proved difficult, Lee managed to bring the Southern forces together. The outcome did not match the effort, and Lee took responsibility for the failure.

Lee returned to Richmond and confided the story of Cheat Mountain to Davis. The president then understood what the public could not know, and his faith and trust in Lee were unshaken. It was not long before the Union navy attacked and defeated the Confederate forces at Port Royal, South Carolina, gaining in the process a much-needed deep-water port. The command of the Department of South Carolina, Georgia and East Florida was given to General Lee, who immediately set about improving the coastal defenses.

Beyond the need to build forts and earthworks, Lee had to organize the chaos of state volunteers, state politicians and the constant reality of the

South's martial resources. By early 1862, Lee was overwhelmed by the need to do so much with so little. Command of an actual army eluded Lee; instead, he remained at the disposal of President Davis.

In January 1862, Lee visited his father's grave on Cumberland Island, Georgia. It was the first such visit, but it would not be the last. Lee was drawn by an inquisitive desire to define himself in relationship to "Light Horse Harry" Lee. The elder Lee had fled the country in the wake of financial and social ruin, and Lee never saw his father again. Unlike his father, General Lee would not abandon his duties and responsibilities for impulsive self-centered motives. His family, his men and the Old Dominion remained at the center of his attention, and he would persevere. The pilgrimage left Lee with a confidence that would strengthen him and inspire those whom he commanded.

In March 1862, a series of devastating setbacks to the Confederate cause prompted Davis to recall Lee to Richmond. Finding himself on President Davis's staff yet a third time would prove utterly dejecting for Lee. He could not know that his destiny was being shaped by events only seven miles away from the Confederate capital.

In June of that year, at the Battle of Seven Pines, commanding General Joseph E. Johnston was badly wounded. His second in command, General Gustavus Smith, could not articulate to President Davis a clear plan for the next day's battle. Frustrated, Davis gave over command of the army to Lee, and the fate of the Southern Republic would become Lee's direct responsibility.

This book will focus on General Lee's first year of service to the Confederacy. During his lifetime and since, much has been offered in the way of praise, criticism and outright challenges to certain actions and decisions made by General Lee during this time. The context in which such actions and decisions occurred lends understanding to Lee's unique perspective. General Robert E. Lee was, after all, a unique character in an epic struggle crowded with generals, some of whom were reactionary, ineffective or just plain bad. Lee's method of cooperative command, after much careful and personal introspection, took into consideration the goal to be achieved, the importance of that goal and the ultimate cost of attaining that goal.

Taken from memoirs, letters, newspapers, veteran's journals and official records of the war, a compelling story unfolds. Told often through first-person accounts, the drama of General Lee's first year shows how skillfully he utilized the barest resources and manpower to their full advantage.

The diary of Mary Boykin Chesnut is quoted in each chapter to reflect the sentiments and emotions of those not directly involved in the fighting.

Her husband, James Chesnut, would eventually be promoted to brigadier general, providing Mary with information from the battlefields upon which she could reflect. Her diary takes in the entire epic of the Civil War and gives a provocative look at everyday life in the South during that time.

Today, Robert E. Lee is a Southern icon. He has been the subject of thousands of discourses exploring what he did, how he did it and why. This does not mean that Lee does not merit further consideration. In particular, his own words go far in bringing meaning and understanding to his actions.

CHAPTER 1

Mustering the Troops

Already they begin to cry out for more ammunition, and already the blockade is beginning to shut it all out.
—*Mary Boykin Chesnut, July 16, 1861*

Loyalty is an envious virtue. When hostilities began between the North and the South, Robert E. Lee was an officer in the United States Army. The Union courted Lee with impressive offers, but Lee was a Virginia man first and foremost. On the day after Virginia seceded from the Union, Lee declined to continue in the Federal service. In a letter to General Winfield Scott on April 20, 1861, Lee wrote, "Save in defense of my native state, I never desire again to draw my sword."

The previous January, while commanding the Department of Texas from Fort Mason, Lee had written to his distant cousin Martha Custis Williams. In words rich with patriotic spirit, Lee had addressed the forthcoming conflict and stated clearly his allegiance. To "Markie," he wrote:

> *I hope you have seen Lolo often since his return & receive good news from Orton. My letters from home frequently mention him & in one of the last it was stated that he & Custis were looking forward to captaincies in the Army of the Southern Republic! The subject recalls my grief at the condition of our country. God alone can save us from our folly, selfishness & short sightedness. The last accounts seem to show that we have barely escaped anarchy to be plunged into civil war. What will be the result I cannot conjecture. I only see that a fearful calamity is upon us & fear that the country will have to pass through for its sins a fiery ordeal. I am unable to realize that our people will destroy a government inaugurated by the blood & wisdom of our patriot*

fathers, that has given us peace & prosperity at home, power & security abroad & under which we have acquired a colossal strength unequalled in the history of mankind. I wish to live under no other government, & there is no sacrifice I am not ready to make for the preservation of the Union save that of honour. If a disruption takes place I shall go back in sorrow to my people & share the misery of my native state & save in her defence there will be one soldier less in the world than now. I wish to for no other flag than the "Star Spangled Banner," & no other air than "Hail Columbia."

Lee's historical sense of the nation was that America was well worth the efforts and sacrifices of the revolutionaries. His own father had become famous fighting the British. Men Lee emulated, George Washington foremost, had risked everything for a country that was now ripping at the seams. Yet, above all, like generations before him, Lee placed his homeland of Virginia first in duty and honor.

On April 12, 1861, at four thirty in the morning, the schism became a fact of history the Rebels began their bombardment of Fort Sumter in Charleston Harbor. On April 23, 1861, the same day that George McClellan was named major general over Ohio's volunteers, Brigadier General Lee was given full command of Virginia's military. In this role, General Lee functioned as the organizer of an army, not as a field commander. Under Lee's guidance, thousands of recruits were eventually equipped, drilled and readied for action.

In preparing Virginia for war, Lee knew full well that no force he mustered could conquer the North. He had been a member of the Federal army for so long that he knew the strength of its manufacturing facilities and the size of the population from which it could draw troops.

What he knew he could do was to successfully defend Virginia from invasion. To Daniel Ruggles, commander of Rappahannock River Defenses, Lee wrote on April 24, 1861: "You will act on the defensive, station your troops at suitable points to command the railroads." Lee had full confidence in Ruggles, a brigadier general of Virginia Volunteers, West Point graduate and veteran of the Mexican War.

Virginia's forces were volunteers and, like Lee himself, ready to do whatever was necessary to defend their homeland. Lee promoted their patriotism and dedication to a cause both noble and grand. He spoke foremost to the honor of Virginia. Bonded by this sentiment, against a common foe, the assembly of an army began.

Manpower would initially be drawn from standing militia units, which numbered over 100,000 across Virginia. The state had a long militia tradition that dated back to the American Revolution. Next came the volunteers, of which

Mustering the Troops

The "Stone Wall": General T.J. Jackson. *Courtesy of Douglas W. Bostick.*

there was no shortage. Lee established a series of recruitment centers across the state, where companies could be raised at the local level. The command structure would take shape as each company elected its officers. Once brought to camp around Richmond, these companies would form into regiments.

Major Thomas J. Jackson had served as a professor of physics and as artillery instructor at Virginia Military Institute. Prone to bizarre rituals and rooted in a determined Presbyterian faith, Jackson was thought of as a natural leader, capable and determined, almost to a fault.

On April 27, Lee wrote to Jackson, outlining his preference for organization of the units:

> *You will proceed, without delay, to Harper's Ferry, Virginia, in execution of the orders of the governor of the State, and assume command of that post. After mustering into the service of the State such companies as may be accepted under your instructions, you will organize them into regiments or battalions, uniting, as far as possible, companies from the same section of the State. These will be placed under their senior captains, until field officers can be appointed by the governor.*

The organizational structure of the army that Lee chose greatly contributed to its future success. Rather than build an army at corps strength, Lee emphasized the mobility of an army of brigades. Lee knew the armies of the North were big but slow because of their size; tens of thousands of troops and thousands of wagons could not outmaneuver one quick and effective battalion.

The men arrived in camp wearing every possible combination of uniform. Some wore blue, some gray, some blue and red and some butternut. Plumes and rosettes decorated their hats, and many wore fancy sashes and gloves. Boots and brass shined in the sun, as did the contagious smiles of the recruits as they met men from locales previously unknown. Here, common cause united shoemakers, bankers and farmers. Family members turned to the home tasks of knitting socks and sewing the regimental flags. Women's Relief Societies began gathering scrap cloth for bandages and raising money for medical supplies.

The work of building defenses continued to require General Lee's attention. On April 29, Lee wrote to Colonel Andrew Talcott, a Virginia railroad engineer. Talcott, a West Point graduate, was now sixty-four years of age, but he was eager to serve as the chief engineer for the State of Virginia.

Lee's directives provided for improved river defenses:

> *You will proceed up James River, to the vicinity of Burwell's Bay, & select the most suitable point which, in your judgement, should be fortified, in order to prevent the ascent of the river by the enemy…you will then proceed to the mouth of the Appomattox, and there perform the same service, selecting some point below the mouth of that river…*

Lee's letter to Talcott is indicative of the manner in which Lee gave orders. Lee could not presume to know specifically where to situate a fort, so he deferred to Talcott's abilities to make a decision and build upon it. General Lee's deference to his subordinates was a hallmark of his military career. Acting otherwise, Lee could appear to others to be arrogant and assuming, traits not consistent with his sense of being a gentleman or a general.

On April 30, 1861, Lee wrote to his wife about the age of so many of the eager recruits. Lee observed:

> *That I could not consent to take boys from their schools and young men from their colleges and put them in the ranks at the beginning of the war when they are not needed. The war may last ten years. Where are our ranks to be filled from then?*

The Richmond training center was named "Camp Lee" after R.E. Lee's father. Cadets from Virginia Military Institute served as drillmasters. Major Jackson was now assigned to supervise these cadets as they carried out their duties. Each cadet worked to teach the basics of drill formation, trying to instill some semblance of military bearing in each new soldier. In just four weeks, seventeen regiments had been formed. It was only a matter of time before their ranks began to dwindle, not from a hail of Yankee bullets, but from disease.

Calvin Conner, a member of South Carolina's Catawba Rifles, wrote home from Manassas junction:

There is but one thing I fear much and that is sickness which is rapidly increasing in our ranks. There is more sickness in our regiment at this time than there has been…and there has been several deaths for which as I said before we ought to be thankful that we have escaped so far without being called to render up our account at the bar of God away from amidst the many kind and loved ones at home. I often feel sad when I see a poor soldier lying upon his blanket with none of the many comforts of which he has been used to at home for I know that they must feel bad. They have no one to feel and care for them in the camp amongst strangers who can fill the place of a kind and affectionate mother or sister, and I fear there are a great many that never know how to appreciate their kind until now.

As he reviewed the new troops who were able-bodied, Lee was optimistic that soon they may even have a rifle to carry. The Federal arsenals that had been seized provided some rifles that were suitable for combat, most being the .69-caliber smoothbore musket, but there were not nearly enough for everyone. State supplies consisted of antiquated flintlocks, dating from the previous century.

The difference between a flintlock and a musket using a primer cap was tremendous on the battlefield. A soldier could reasonably expect to get off three rounds per minute with the .69 caliber; with a flintlock, one round per minute was usually the case.

Lee wrote to Major Francis M. Boykin Jr., directing the distribution of these arms. General Lee instructed Boykin accordingly:

To enable you to supply any deficiency in arms in the companies, 200 muskets of the old pattern, flint-locks, will be forwarded by Col. Jackson, the commanding officer at Harper's Ferry, to your order, from whence you must take measures to receive them & convey them to their destination, under guard, if necessary. I regret that no other arms are at present for issue.

Later in May, Lee instructed Jackson to offer a bounty for muskets: "You are authorized to offer the payment of $5 a piece for each musket that may be returned of those taken possession of by the people in and about Harper's Ferry." Apparently, during the seizure of the arsenal by Southern troops, several of the precious rifles fell into the hands of local citizens.

For heavy artillery, there were hundreds of big guns at the naval yard at Norfolk that had been seized by Virginia's troops. Among them were many rifled Dahlgren guns, artillery highly effective against enemy ships and fortifications. The foundries and shipbuilding and repair facilities were also at the disposal of the Confederacy. Lee directed the manufacture of tons of gunpowder, while blacksmiths turned to making bayonets.

For the cavalry, there were plenty of horses, but no pistols or sabers. These would have to come from England until Southern armories could catch up with orders. Lee knew that an army must be mobile, and that would take wagons, hundreds of them, to support the needs of an army on the march. While more were made, wagons were sometimes commandeered to get the job done. Next, Lee turned to the immediate need of each man in arms: food.

The state of food preservation in 1861 consisted mostly of smoking meat or preserving it with salt. Pickled vegetables were often compromised by poor corking, which allowed air in, thus spoiling the goods. Canning was not an accomplished art, and often the cans of rations turned rancid in transit. The one staple component of a soldier's diet—bread—came mostly in the form of a perforated biscuit known as "hardtack." Regrettably, many a man on both sides of the battle line was forced to make a meal of only this one commodity, and then only after soaking it in water to loosen up the worms so they could first be removed.

Lee would make good use of foragers, who would help his men live off the land. If the land failed them, then it would be an unfortunate part of war to have to take from people's stores as they moved through populated areas. Later in the war, soldiers would find that for a starving army, there was only the finest line between paying useless Confederate money for chickens and outright pilferage.

Soon, the Virginia troops for which Lee was responsible were transferred to the War Department's supervision, leaving Lee effectively out of a job. Lee then served as President Davis's advisor. Acting at times on his own and without official directive, Lee oversaw the reinforcement of defensive earthworks around Richmond. He wrote of his activities to his wife:

> *I have just returned from a visit to the batteries and troops on James and York rivers, etc., where I was some days...Yesterday I turned over to it the command of the military and naval forces of the State, in accordance with the proclamation of the Government and the agreement between the State*

Mary Custis Lee. *Courtesy of Douglas W. Bostick.*

and the Confederate States. I do not know what my position will be. I should like to retire to private life, if I could be with you and the children, but if I can be of any service to the State or her cause I must continue.

On this same date, Lee wrote again to Colonel Jackson. The letter betrays Lee's concern for the necessary implements of war:

In your preparation for the defense of your position, it is considered advisable not to intrude upon the soil of Maryland, unless compelled by the necessities of war. The aid of its citizens might be obtained in that quarter. I regret I have no engineer of experience to send you...I have directed that four 6-pound guns be forwarded to you as soon as possible, and two 12 pound howitzers, with a supply of ammunition and equipment for firing, will be sent to you at once. There are no caissons. Horses, wagons & harness will be procured near you by an agent of the quartermaster's department...flour & provisions for use of the troops must be secured...I have directed that one thousand muskets, obtained from North Carolina, be sent to you, to aid in arming your command.

Lack of shelter for the new troops became an annoyance when rain threatened. On May 10, Lee addressed this issue with Colonel George H. Terrett, a former United States marine:

For this purpose, it will be necessary to remove them from the towns, if possible, & establish them in camps, where their constant instruction and discipline can be attended to. They will the sooner become familiar with the necessities of service, & be better prepared for its hardships. It will be impossible to furnish tents at this time, but it is hoped that unoccupied buildings or temporary plank huts might be obtained where needed.

Lee's concern for the continued regimentation of the new troops echoed in a letter two days later to General Walter Gwynn, who in late April had received a new mount from the citizens of Petersburg, Virginia. Lee admonished Gwynn: "Apply all your means & use every exertion to the instruction & discipline of your men, & prepare them for hard and active service…"

Also on May 12, Lee wrote again to Jackson; his words provided a sobering, yet realistic, assessment of Virginia's military resources:

We have no rifles or cavalry equipments. The latter may use double-barreled shot-guns & buck-shot, if no better arms can be procured…You know our limited resources, & must abstain from all provocation for attack as long as possible.

Lee was commissioned as a general in the Confederate army on May 14, the day that the Confederate Congress asked President Davis to proclaim a national day of fasting and prayer. On May 15, Lee's letter to Colonel Terrett foreshadowed an engagement soon to come:

I have requested Col. Cocke to fill up Col. Garland's regiment, stationed at Manassas Junction, from companies called by him into the service of the State, and, as soon as he can organize other regiments, to send such reinforcements to that point as he may deem necessary or you require. It will be necessary for you to give particular attention to the defense of that point, & to organize your force in front of it, to oppose, as far as your means will allow, any advance into the country from Washington.

To General Milledge L. Bonham, a former congressman, Lee asserted again his policy of strict defense. On May 22, Lee wrote:

I need not call the attention of one as experienced as yourself to the necessity of preventing the troops from all interference with the rights and property of the citizens of the State, & of enforcing rigid discipline & obedience to orders. But it is proper for me to state to you that the policy of the State at present is strictly defensive. No attack, or provocation for attack will therefore be given, but every attack resisted to the extent of your means.

By May 24, Union troops occupied two key Virginia cities, Alexandria and Arlington. This same day, Lee instructed Bonham:

> *Send an express to Colonel* [Eppa] *Hunton, at Leesburg, to destroy all the bridges of the Loudoun and Hampshire Railroad as far down towards Alexandria as possible, and to keep you and General* [Joseph E.] *Johnston advised of the movements of the enemy towards Harper's Ferry.*

General Lee's thoughts turned to family and home. By Providence, Lee's wife and daughters had left Arlington days before. The thought of enemy troops on lands held so dearly and for so long by his wife's family was almost incomprehensible.

Lee confessed in heartfelt tones his own shortcomings. He wrote to Mrs. Lee on May 25:

> *I sympathize deeply with your feelings at leaving your dear home. I have experienced them myself & they are constantly revived. I fear we have not been grateful enough for the happiness there within…I acknowledge… my ingratitude, my transgressions & my unworthiness, & submit with resignation to what He thinks proper to inflict upon me. We must trust all there to Him & I do not think it prudent or right for you to return there, while the U.S. troops occupy that country.*

Arlington, ancestral home to Mary Custis Lee. *Courtesy of Douglas W. Bostick.*

In the early days of mobilization, men's emotions were drawn between one's state and the new Confederacy. For some governors, it was not clear what this new government could or would do for the men raised and trained at the local level. It became Lee's responsibility to address these concerns, as a letter to Georgia Governor Joseph E. Brown illustrates. In a style that was respectful to the position Brown held, Lee stated the obvious in terms to which the governor could respond without taking Lee's words as a rebuke. In fact, Brown, who clashed with President Davis over the authority of a confederated government, had sent his men to face the enemy unarmed.

On the twenty-sixth of May, Lee observed:

> *I deem it proper to call your attention to the fact that many of the volunteer companies from your State have arrived at Richmond without arms. The demand upon Virginia has been so great that all arms have been exhausted, except the old flint-lock muskets. It is apprehended that the troops thus provided will not do themselves justice, opposed to an enemy whose arms are so much superior. I thought it probable that you would like to provide the men of your State with such better arms as may be at your disposal, and therefore take the liberty of bringing this matter to your notice…if, then, you have to spare any pistols, carbines, or equipments for that army, you would greatly further the common cause by sending them to Richmond.*

Only a few days before, the Confederate government had moved to Richmond, a difficult place to defend due to the proximity of several river ways. Lee continued employing his defensive strategy of placing heavy guns to reinforce the line, tending all the while to the heavy load of administrative chores, as well.

Still, there was a vagueness of General Lee's actual position that troubled him. As commander of Virginia's state forces, the mandate was clear. As a general of the Confederacy, much was demanded, yet Lee had only certain authority with which to dispatch and delegate. Davis had insisted on maintaining direct control of the troops but came frequently to Lee for advice.

Davis was quick to exploit Lee's complete knowledge of Virginia's geography and defense works, depending on Lee's engineering experience to resourcefully prepare the state for action. Lee enjoyed the company of Lieutenant Walter Taylor, who served as Lee's aid throughout the war, and Lieutenant Colonel Augustine Washington, the late president's great-nephew. These officers supported Lee in a role that he could not fully understand, especially in light of Mrs. Lee's letter mentioning her husband's appointment as Confederate commander-in-chief.

Mustering the Troops

President Jefferson Davis. *Courtesy of the Library of Congress.*

In the second week of June, Lee wrote to his beloved wife of his confusion and frustration:

> *I am anxious to get into the field, but am detained by matters beyond my control. I have never heard of the appointment, to which you allude, of Commander-in-Chief of the Confederate States Army, nor have I any expectation or wish for it. President Davis holds that position. Since the transfer of the military operations in Virginia to the authorities of the Confederate States, I have only occupied the position of a general in that service, with the duties devolved on me by the President. I have been labouring to prepare and get into the field the Virginia troops, and to strengthen, by those from the other States, the threatened commands of Johnston, Beauregard, Huger, Garnett, etc. Where I shall go I do not know, as that will depend upon President Davis. As usual, in getting through with a thing, I have broken down a little and had to take my bed last evening, but am at my office this morning and hope will soon be right again...*

Near the end of the month, certain events would combine to distract Lee's attention. On June 25, Lee received a report from General Robert S. Garnett, who was in the western region of Virginia. Garnett had succeeded in bringing together over five thousand ragtag recruits and had regimented them into a properly disciplined unit. He went on to report that most of the locals in the western counties did not favor the Confederate cause. With Union armies on the move, Garnett was in desperate need of support. Lee sent Garnett three regiments of reinforcements.

The Virginia governor, realizing Garnett's predicament, rode out to meet with him, accompanied by heavily armed militiamen. Confederate Captain Greenlee Davis wrote of his travel with Governor John Letcher as they rode together:

> *We are splendidly mounted and heavily armed. The Governor carries two heavy six-shooters. General Coleman carries two revolvers, two pocket pistols, and a double barrel gun, I carry two heavy six shooters and our orderly carries two holster pistols.*

On July 11, Garnett was demoralized as Rich Mountain fell to Federal General William Starke Rosecrans, whose men were part of an army of over twenty thousand commanded by George McClellan. An earlier skirmish near the town of Philippi had drawn an exaggerated, but positive, response from the North.

Two days later, Garnett lay dead near Carrick's Ford on the Cheat River. General McClellan's forces had pursued Garnett's retreat and felled the Rebel general in a skirmish with the rear guard. In death, Garnett became the first general of either side to be killed in action during the war.

Artillerist E.P. Alexander recalled Garnett's audacity:

> *Had he lived I am sure he would have been one of our great generals. He lost his life in a characteristic manner…with ten of his men who were raw troops he had halted to delay the enemy at a creek crossing…under a sharp fire…Garnett remarked they needed "a little example." He stood in full view of the enemy and walked slowly back and forth, a target for the sharpshooters. He was presently shot dead.*

Lee received word of Garnett's demise the next day. Garnett had been Lee's lone staff member in April, having been appointed adjutant general. This early role had endeared Garnett to Lee, and this bond made the loss all the more sorrowful.

Lee ordered General John B. Floyd and General Henry A. Wise to support the remnants of Garnett's army and placed General W.W. Loring in charge, with special orders to guard the rail lines. Lee did not know at the time that these three men would soon present him with one of the greatest challenges to his talent and tact as a leader of men.

CHAPTER 2

Yankees on the Run

Dr. Gibbs says the faces of the dead grow as black as charcoal on the battlefield and they shine in the sun.
—Mary Boykin Chesnut, July 22, 1861

By July 17, Davis had turned Lee's attention to Manassas. Rebel spies had reported that the Yankee army was on the move. Just days before, Calvin Conner wrote to his family of the apprehensions shared by the men in camp:

> *We may expect before long to be brought face to face with our enemy unless there is a compromise affected by Congress which is now in Session for which we can hardly hope when we look over the list of names that compose that body. Preparations are still going on rapidly at Manassas and other places for the reception of the enemy, and I think that we will be able to give them a warm one at any time…*

Federal General Irvin McDowell had by now brought his army toward the Manassas railroad junction. Facing off against them was the Confederate Army of the Potomac, commanded by P.G.T. Beauregard, one of McDowell's classmates at West Point. The Army of the Shenandoah, commanded by General Joseph E. Johnston, was in transit. Johnston, also a West Pointer, had experienced combat in both the Seminole Wars and the Mexican War.

A strategy conference was held by Johnston and Beauregard on the evening of July 20; the decision was made to attack the Federal left with a right flanking action. By the twenty-first, the battle was about to commence.

Thousands of frolicking onlookers had come to Manassas from Washington. Some came for a picnic, but many others were intent upon witnessing the decisive battle of this short-fought war. Children played about as parents broke open bottles of champagne and feasted on fine foods. Crowds cheered as the armies, under the Stars and Stripes, moved up to the line. The sense of slaughter and suffering had not yet overcome the menagerie as the two armies pushed closer to each other. On both sides, the colors of the regimental flags and banners were brilliantly displayed.

Confederate veteran Major James B. Steedman, of South Carolina Pea Ridge Volunteers, wrote of the pending engagement:

> *The morning of the 21st of June* [July] *began clear and tranquil and promised as peaceful a Sabbath day as ever rose to remind resting man of the goodness of his Master. During the previous night, however, there were sounds in the air, the crashing of artillery, wheels as they were dragged into position, and the tramp of armed hosts marching up to their allotted posts, which convinced us that this calm was treacherous, and that the day was to witness stormy scenes.*

Confusion was the order of the day as each side attempted a flanking attack—the Rebel right against the Union left, the Union right against the Confederate left—in such a swirl of smoke and confusion that both armies together resembled a dog chasing its tail. Having yet to practice at war, both armies stumbled, fought and stumbled again.

A promising Yankee move on the Confederate left was checked after General N.G. Evans pushed some of his men into place until the Rebel line could adjust to a redirected Yankee assault. Johnston's last troops came up in time, and soon the Federals were withdrawing.

Though neither could know it at the time, Confederate Generals Bernard Bee and Jackson were soon to become legendary. Jackson would fight on, but Bee would die on the field of battle. Bee's line had begun to falter when, upon seeing Jackson steadfast in the fight, he told his men to stand like that "stonewall."

The Union army was swept back toward Washington, entangled with the mass of civilians whose party was now over. Sickened at the sight of the dead and wounded, women fell into a faint of emotion as their husbands threw back gulps of whiskey and prodded their horses along. Soon, the road was bogged down with sightseers, ambulances and artillery wagons. After a night of rain, the victorious Rebels rested, feasting on the abandoned turkeys and hams left by the panicked citizens.

President Davis, who had taken a special train to watch the fight, wrote on the night of the twenty-first: "We have won a glorious though dear bought victory. Night closed on the enemy in full flight and closely pursued."

Lee was not on the field at Manassas; Davis had directed him to remain in the capital. Lee's mood was melancholy and subdued. To his wife, he wrote:

> *That indeed was a glorious victory, and has lightened the pressure upon our front amazingly. Do not grieve for the brave dead. Sorrow for those they left behind—friends, relatives and families. The former are at rest. The latter must suffer. The battle will be repeated there in greater force. I hope God will again smile on us and strengthen our hearts and arms. I wished to partake in the former struggle, and am mortified by my absence. But the president thought it more important I should be here. I could not have done as well as had been done, but I could have helped, and taken part in the struggle for my home and neighborhood. So the work is done, I care not by whom it is done.*

The Virginia forces that fought at Manassas were organized and trained by Lee but commanded by Beauregard and Johnston. These generals assumed a high point in Southern public opinion, while General Lee, who suffered the poor health and temperament of President Davis better than most, continued to work in a supporting role.

Disease had claimed one of the president's eyes, and he also suffered from facial spasms and chronic stomach ailments. Such debilities predisposed Davis to an ill temper, but Lee had become quite adept at working with the president, despite his occasional fits.

Davis, in turn, knew General Lee's power of persuasion and his tolerance of difficult personalities. Since the beginning of the war, Davis had held Lee in high regard and kept him close when his trusted advice was most needed. Davis could work with Lee because he knew Lee was not a self-seeking person.

President Davis intended to fully utilize the best Lee had to offer as he turned to the ongoing dilemma of competing commands in western Virginia. Lee's previous orders had apparently been tempered by the inability of Wise and Floyd to get along. Federal General McClellan had by now seeded his command to Rosecrans, and it was clear that the Union was anticipating an offensive. If not united in command, the Confederate forces could not withstand attack.

In sending Lee to western Virginia, Davis hoped that Loring, Floyd and Wise would accept the visiting general as mediator and not feel insulted or threatened by his presence. Unfortunately, none of the three knew General Lee as the president did, and their lack of appreciation for Lee's character would serve only to undermine the upcoming campaign.

CHAPTER 3

In the Shadow of Cheat Mountain

A hospital nurse from North Carolina says she likes everything confederate but the "assisting surgeons." She does not "like their ways." They take the white sugar and give the patients moist brown…and as for the whiskey, brandy etc., many a man has died because the surgeon did not leave from his own toddy whiskey enough to keep a typhoid case alive.
—Mary Boykin Chesnut, August 29, 1861

In late July, Lee made the journey to western Virginia, determined to facilitate the compromises desired by Davis. Lee's mission was not to take command, but to bring the two commands together. He traveled to the mountains with just his cook Meredith, his manservant Perry, Colonel Washington and Captain Taylor.

One Confederate soldier, upon seeing Lee for the first time, was rather taken by his looks:

> *He wore the uniform of a Federal Colonel, his old rank. His hair was very dark with only a chance gray hair. He was closely shaven, and had a square-cut coal-black moustache…there was a kindness in his expression most unusual in one possessing eyes so dark and brilliant. He was dignified and courtly without any of the "hauteur" naturally acquired by command.*

Many westerners were not friends of the new government in Richmond. The western counties of Virginia had long felt they were relegated to second-place consideration by the state's legislature. Further, there were fewer slaves in the western counties, whereas slaves east of the Alleghenies counted three-fifths of a person each, which gave the eastern portion of the state a three-seat majority in the national Congress.

Such antagonism fueled resentment among these people, most of whom just wanted to be left alone, and the conflict taken elsewhere. The nullification of the secession ordinance was soon a growing topic of discussion.

Loring was wary of Lee, whom he had outranked in the Mexican War. His perception of Lee's mission was one of meddling and imposition. Unlike General Lee, Loring had not graduated from West Point, having enlisted as a soldier during the Seminole War. He was a lifelong bachelor, lawyer and former state legislator who, during the Mexican War, lost an arm at Chapultepec.

Wise was an experienced politician and had been governor of Virginia when John Brown went to the gallows. He had also served as a foreign ambassador.

Floyd was a graduate of South Carolina College and also a former Virginia governor who later served as secretary of war under President James Buchanan. Political rivals, Wise and Floyd detested each other.

Lee lacked any official authority to command and found the work of mediation exhausting. Lee's letters to Wise are reflective of the frustration Lee felt over Wise's refusal to coordinate with Floyd, to the point of requesting that his legion be separated from Floyd, creating yet another independent body of Southern troops. To Lee, the subdivision of such a small force would undermine its effectiveness against the Yankees. On August 8, Lee wrote to Wise:

> In regard to the request to separate the commands of Genl Floyd & yourself, & to assign to each respective fields of action, it would, in my opinion, be contrary to the purpose of the President, & destroy the prospect of the success of the campaign in Kanawha District. Our enemy is so strong at all points that we can only hope to give him an effective blow by a concentration of our forces, & that this may be done surely & rapidly, their movements & actions must be controlled by one head. I hope, therefore, that as soon as your command can move forward, in the preparation for which I feel assured no time will be lost, that you will join Genl Floyd, & take that part in the campaign which may be assigned your brigade.

On August 21, Lee had to again lecture Wise on the nature of cooperation, especially during a time of war:

> The necessities of war require the organization of the forces to be adapted to the service to be performed, & sometimes brigades & separate commands have to be remodeled accordingly. This must be done in accordance with the judgement of the commanding officer. The transmission of orders to

*troops through their immediate commanders is in accordance with usage
& propriety. Still, there are occasions when this can not be conformed to
without detriment to the service.*

Lee was compelled to visit the camps of each general in order to assess
the condition of the troops. Lee found the men disorganized, ill-equipped
and sick. He moved about, visiting and encouraging, always firm but sincere.
The overall condition of the men distressed him greatly.

In early August, Lee wrote to his wife about the pitiful condition of so
many of the Southern troops:

*The points from which we can be attacked are numerous, and their means
are unlimited. So we must always be on the alert. My uneasiness on these
points brought me out here. It is so difficult to get our people, unaccustomed
to the necessities of war, to comprehend and promptly execute the measures
required for the occasion…The soldiers everywhere are sick. The measles
are prevalent throughout the whole army, and you know that disease leaves
unpleasant results, attacks on the lungs, typhoid, etc., especially in camp,
where accommodations for the sick are poor.*

In a later letter to his two daughters, General Lee wrote:

*My precious daughters…it rains here all the time literally. There has
not been sunshine enough since my arrival to dry my clothes. Perry is my
washerman, and socks and towel suffer. But the worst of the rain is that the
ground has become so saturated with water that the constant travel on the
roads has made them almost impassable, so that I cannot get up sufficient
supplies for the troops to move.*

On August 27, Lee responded to a letter from Wise dated the twenty-
fourth. The tone suggested Lee's irritation with Wise's continued efforts at
manipulation and control:

*Am much concerned at the view you take of your position & its effect upon
your legion. I do not apprehend the consequences you suppose will follow
from its being under the general orders of the commander of the Army of the
Kanawha…the Army of the Kanawha is too small for active & successful
operation to be divided at present. I beg, therefore, for the sake of the cause
you have so much at heart, you will permit no division of sentiment or
action to disturb its harmony or arrest its efficiency.*

A month had passed, and still Wise did not see things Lee's way. Fortuitously, Wise soon received orders to Richmond, leaving Floyd no one with whom to quarrel.

On August 31, Lee's appointment as a full general in the service of the Confederacy was confirmed. The next day, at Cape Girardeau, Missouri, Ulysses S. Grant took command. That September 1, Lee wrote to Mrs. Lee:

> *Those on the sick-list would form an army. The measles is still among them, though I hope it is dying out...The constant cold rains, with no shelter but tents, have aggravated it. All these drawbacks, with impassable roads, have paralysed our efforts.*

Lee, accompanied by his son William Henry Fitzhugh Lee's cavalry, had reconnoitered the terrain, searching for any way to take Cheat Mountain and thus control the Parkersburg Turnpike. Both Lee and his son, known as "Rooney," sensed that Loring had spent an inordinate amount of time fretting over supply lines and other logistics, ignoring the fact that expediency was the key to a successful attack. In his stead, Lee began to consider a number of options, choosing to follow the suggestion of one of his officers.

On September 12, the troops under the command of Colonel Albert Rust were directed to engage the Union pickets in the rear. Rust was a former state legislator and national congressman; he had earned the honor of leading off the attack after finding a narrow passage through the overgrown mountainside. As a point of honor, Lee then deferred to Rust in consideration of his efforts. The opening shots would be the signal for the other Confederate forces to push forward.

This plan of attack, though tactically sound, was complicated and required close coordination. The objective, the crest of Cheat Mountain, was held by Union Colonel Nathan Kimball and his regiments from Indiana and Ohio. The sum total of the Northern force was about eighteen hundred men.

Brigadier General William M'Comb recalled what happened next:

> *Our instructions were that, when our troops on the east side of Cheat Mountain commenced firing, we were to charge the fortifications in the rear from the west...The plan was an admirable one. General Reynolds had no intimation that we were in the rear...the command on the east side of the mountain never fired a shot. It was impossible to communicate with them. So the expedition was a complete failure, although well planned and, up to this point, a complete success.*

Rumors at the time suggested that Rust had been duped by captured Federal pickets, who told his staff that the position held five times the actual number of defenders. Seeing any attack as now futile, he simply withdrew.

One can only imagine the drawn, weary face of General Lee as he pulled his old blue coat over his shoulders. Again, Lee would search for answers, yet blame no one. The honor of his young officer was at stake, and of this trait Lee had said: "There is a true glory and a true honor, the glory of duty done, the honor of the integrity of principle."

To his life confidante, he spoke, on September 17:

> *I received, dear Mary, your letter of the 5ᵗʰ by Beverly Turner, who is a nice young soldier. I am pained to see fine young men like him, of education and standing, from all the old and respectable families in the State, serving in the ranks. I hope in time they will receive their reward. I met him as I was returning from an expedition to the enemy's works, which I had hoped to have surprised on the morning of the 12ᵗʰ, both at Cheat Mountain and on Valley River. All the attacking parties with great labour had reached their destination, over mountains considered impassable to bodies of troops, notwithstanding a heavy storm that set in the day before and raged all night, which they had to stand till daylight. Their arms were then unserviceable, and they in poor condition for a fierce assault against artillery and superior numbers. After waiting till 10 o'clock for the assault on Cheat Mountain, which did not take place, and which was to have been the signal for the rest, they were withdrawn, and after waiting three days in front of the enemy, hoping he would come out of his trenches, we returned to our position at this place. I can not tell you my regret and mortification at the untoward events that caused the failure of the plan. I had taken every precaution to ensure success and counted on it. But the Ruler of the Universe willed otherwise and sent a storm to disconcert a well-laid plan, and to destroy my hopes. We are no worse off now than before, except the disclosure of our plan, against which they will guard.*

Soon, the Virginia governor would ask for an explanation from Lee, having heard of the perceived failure on his part to take the fight to Reynolds. In deference to no one, and with a mind to keep responsibility for any failure close to his own soul, General Lee responded to Governor Lecter:

> *I was very sanguine of taking the enemy's works on last Thursday morning. I had considered the subject well. With great effort the troops intended for the surprise had reached their destination, having traversed twenty miles of*

steep, rugged mountain paths; and the last day through a terrible storm, which lasted all night, and in which they had to stand drenched to the skin in cold rain. Still, their spirits were good. When morning broke, I could see the enemy's tents on Valley River, at the point on the Huttonsville road just below me. It was a tempting sight. We waited for the attack on Cheat Mountain, which was to be the signal. Till 10 a.m. the men were cleaning their unserviceable arms. But the signal did not come. The provisions of the men had been destroyed the preceding day by the storm. They had nothing to eat that morning, could not hold out another day, and were obliged to be withdrawn. The party sent to Cheat Mountain to take that in rear had also to be withdrawn. The attack to come off on the east side failed from the difficulties in the way; the opportunity was lost, and our plan discovered. It is a grievous disappointment to me, I assure you. But for the rainstorm, I have no doubt it would have succeeded. This governor is for your own eye. Please do not speak of it; we must try again.

Victory on the battlefield eluded General Lee for the time being, but later he would have one more chance. By early October, Lee had moved Floyd's army from Meadow Bluff to Wise's position on the eastern crest of Sewell Mountain, with Rosecrans on the opposing crest only a mile away.

Lee's men waited behind strong earthworks for days, but the Federals made no move. As the sun began to brighten the sky on October 6, Lee was crestfallen to find that Rosecrans had withdrawn during the night, choosing to fight another day.

When Lee considered pursuing the Federal force, several of his commanders implored the general to make do. Rations were exhausted and the men were fatigued and cold. General Lee yielded to their protestations, the mere sight of his tired soldiers swaying his resolve to push further. Lee did not know that one of his men, Private E.P. McDonald, had overheard a conversation between Lee and General William E. Starke. Though Starke begged an explanation of the general's failure to chase Rosecrans, Lee's only reply was: "I could not afford to sacrifice the lives of five or six hundred of my people to silence public clamor."

By the end of October 1861, Robert E. Lee had returned to Richmond, where the state capital now served as the capital of the Confederacy. He took the entire Cheat Mountain debacle as his own, mourning the loss of Lieutenant Colonel Washington, who was shot down as he accompanied Rooney on a scouting mission. His disposition upon returning to Richmond was probably best known only to President Davis, in whom Lee had confided. Lee spoke to the president on the condition that no written record be made of the episode, so that no one else would know of Rust's failure.

The
Charleston
Orphan
House.
*Author's
collection.*

It was not long before the general was dubbed "Granny Lee" by the press. Because his previous fame had dimmed in the light of the accomplishments of other Southern commanders, Lee was seen as perhaps too old to command, too unwise or both. Lee had been well aware of the denunciations prior to returning to Richmond.

Private McDonald recalled his observations of Lee and the general's reaction to the public outcry:

> *My quarters being within fifty yards from Lee's tent, I had a good opportunity to study him. When the daily mail came I would pass and re-*

pass his quarters to see the effect of the press and the public clamor against him. He would frequently sit for an hour in the cold autumn sun on a large log near his tent reading the newspapers. I never observed the least change in his appearance. He was ever the same, quiet, self-possessed gentleman.

Life among the troops in the mountains of Virginia caused many to become enamored of Lee as a "soldier's general." Despite the rain, mud, measles and typhoid, General Lee moved among the men, while other officers sought shelter in their flimsy tents. Lee encouraged even the weakest soldier to take strength. This uncommon bond with the common soldier would endure until Appomattox and beyond.

To mark the October 18, 1861 anniversary of the Charleston Orphan House, inspirational poems were read by one of the children to the assembled crowd. Morbid reminders of a soldier's real plight in war, "Appeal for the Soldiers" appeared in the *Charleston Courier* newspaper and has no author to credit:

Appeal for the Soldier spoken by an orphan, on the anniversary of
October 18th, 1861

I ask a gift, but not for us;
We feel no griefs, we fear no wants;
To live a life exempted thus,
From common ills, your bounty grants;
For us, without a passing care,
The seasons change year after year.
I ask for those who freely give
Their lives upon the tented field,
Who bleed and die that you may live
Unharmed and safe; each heart a shield,
A panoply for you and yours,
A rampart on Potomac's Shores.

Is there an eye, of all I see,
One eye that could undimmed remain,
Or tearless at the agony
Of battle on Manassas' plain,

Where manly forms, defaced and torn,
Caused victory herself to mourn?
She mourned with mingled smiles and tears,
Apart, by stalwart Johnson's side,
At gallant Bartow's dying cheers,
For Bee, his country's hope and pride.
Than these she wept no nobler son
At Salamis or Marathon.

Sick, wounded, now, on beds of pain,
In dreary hospital immured,
Your soldiers seek, but seek in vain,
The wonted aid for this endured;
At home—the hand and voice to cheer.
The loving hearts, are wanted there.
Or on the watch at night they stand,
Exposed to chilling dews and rain,
Or march by day—a chosen band,
To scout the hostile hill and plain;
In tattered cloak and coarse array—
Yet none so bold or blithe as they.

There, in the forest lair, they be,
Mellow leaves their tentless bed,
To catch, with wakeful ear and eye,
The cunning foe's insidious tread,
Then wander at the dawning back,
To join the cheerless bivouac.
For these I ask. Can any pause?
What hand so slow, what heart so cold,
As stop to count, in such a cause,
A petty sum of paltry gold,
When, more than gold can buy, the true
And dauntless soldier gives for you?

Ye gallant hearts of kindred strain,
Say, shall I ask your gifts in vain?
The heaving breast, the flashing eye,
The maiden's starting tear reply.

CHAPTER 4

Ready for War

I do not pretend to go to sleep. How can I? If Anderson does not accept terms-at four-the orders are-he shall be fired upon. I count four-St. Michael chimes. I begin to hope. At half-past four, the heavy booming of a cannon. I sprang out of bed. And on my knees-prostrate-I prayed as I never prayed before.
—Mary Boykin Chestut, April 12, 1861

Lee's time in Richmond would be short. It was October 31, and just a week before, on October 24, the overwhelming number of voters in the western counties of Virginia gave a mandate to form a new state in league with the Union. Barely a week later, on November 5, President Davis selected Lee to serve as commander of a new military district consisting of South Carolina, Georgia and East Florida.

Knowing of Lee only what they had read in the press, each governor in the new district sought reassurance from Davis that Lee was the right man for such a challenging post. On November 6, 1861, Davis telegraphed Florida Governor John Milton concerning Lee's appointment, referring to him as "an officer of the highest ability and reputation."

On November 7, 1861, General Lee arrived in Charleston, the "cradle of secession." Lee made no detailed notes on his journey south. However, not long after the general's arrival, a seventeen-year-old attached to a Virginia artillery unit wrote back to his father about his very first journey outside of his home state. He described many of the sites along the way in lavish detail. Young Joseph Wilmer Turner was part of Leake's Battery of Turner's Artillery. The letter was posted from Garden's Corner, Beaufort District, South Carolina, on December 17, 1861. Lee's impression of the city was likely no less curious or favorable:

Charleston's Zouaves. *Courtesy of Douglas W. Bostick.*

As you approach Charleston, the scenery is beautiful; it is situated between Cooper and Ashley rivers…at Wilmington we had observed a slight change in the climate but here it was oppressive. After a late breakfast we walked town to see what was to be seen. After passing through the market and noticing the various vegetables and the tame buzzards that were kept around the market to keep the streets clean, we passed on down Market Street to the wharf. These buzzards resemble the vulture more than those of Virginia and the S-Carolinians have passed a law prohibiting the shooting of them.

At the wharf, we had a fine view of the harbor; directly in front of us some two or three miles was Castle Pinckney situated on a small island; some three or four farther on and almost in the same line was Fort Sumter also on a small island, while away to the left on Sullivan's island we could see the Confederate flag floating over the walls of Fort Moultrie.

Charleston was a port city unrivaled in its political independence and known to sailors since 1670 for its taverns, wenches and debauchery. A certain irony expressed itself as these same sailors entered the harbor and sited first the steeples of St. Michael's and St. Phillip's Episcopal Churches. Closer to the dockage, the twin towers of the Unitarian church and Saint John's Lutheran Church came into view. The gloriously large homes of the wealthy planters and merchants projected proudly from the peninsula's edge. But deep down into the matrix of alleys that bisected the city, life in the shadows could be wild and lusty. Gambling, liquor and prostitution attracted more followers than the best Sunday sermon.

Ready for War

Charleston, 1861. *Courtesy of Douglas W. Bostick.*

Secession from the Union had been preceded by the Democratic National Convention, which was held in Charleston in April 1860. There, Southern delegates squared off with Northern delegates split over the issue of slavery in the territories. The fractioned party could not regroup, and Abraham Lincoln became the first Republican president of the United States. Rebellion was about to become a reality.

On December 18, 1860, the Secession Convention met in Charleston. The purpose of the convention was to legitimize the popular sentiment that had been expressed since the days of John C. Calhoun. He had espoused the right of a state to secede from a union that unfairly taxed or regulated any of its subdivisions. The perception was that a Union led by Lincoln would seek to end slavery in the South. Such a turn of events would devastate the plantation system and disrupt the prevailing social order. On December 20, 1860, the 169 delegates voted to withdraw South Carolina from the United States.

Such a dramatic move as secession did not come without the anticipation of a fight. Thanks to the early efforts of General Bee, local militias had been formed and drilled extensively. Charleston's streets were a parade ground for young recruits. The convention had spoken, and they had answered. The "Sons of the South" were ready for a fight. Now it was up to the Federals to make a move.

Under the cover of darkness on December 26, 1860, Union Major Robert Anderson moved his small force from Fort Moultrie, on Sullivan's Island, to Fort Sumter, situated in the center of Charleston's harbor entrance. Sumter, though not built to completion, afforded better protection than Moultrie and was more defensible. This occupation, without consent of the new Commonwealth of South Carolina, was seen as a provocation.

Above: Charleston celebrates secession. *Courtesy of Douglas W. Bostick.*

Left: The Palmetto State Song. *Courtesy of the Library of Congress.*

South Carolina Volunteers parade past the Charleston Hotel. *Courtesy of Douglas W. Bostick.*

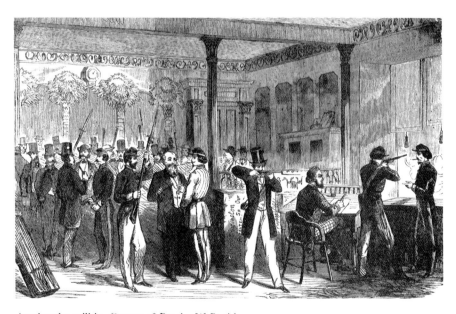

Arming the militia. *Courtesy of Douglas W. Bostick.*

August Dickert, a young member of the Thirty-ninth Battalion of state militia, hurried by train with two of his brothers to join the cause. He described the excitement in the city as talk turned to taking Fort Sumter from the Federals:

> *The city of Charleston was ablaze with excitement, flags waved from the house tops, the heavy tread of the embryo soldiers could be heard in the streets, the corridors of hotels, and in all the public places. The beautiful park on the water front, called the "Battery," was thronged with people of every age and sex, straining their eyes or looking through glasses out at Sumter, whose bristling front was surmounted with cannon, her flags waving defiance.*
>
> *Small boats and steamers dotted the waters of the bay. Ordnance and ammunition were being hurried to the islands. The one continual talk was "Anderson," "Fort Sumter," and "War." While there was no spirit of bravado, or of courting of war, there was no disposition to shirk it. A strict guard was kept at all the wharves, or boat landings, to prevent any espionage on our movements or works. It will be well to say here, that no moment from the day of secession to the day the first gun was fired on Sumter, had been allowed to pass without overtures being made to the government at Washington for a peaceful solution of the momentous question.*

Immediately after the move of Union troops to Sumter, three companies of militia under Colonel J.J. Pettigrew took charge of Castle Pinckney, a smaller horseshoe-shaped fort closer to the Charleston peninsula. Here, the very first flag of secession, a red banner with a white star, was raised over the Federal installation.

Fort Sumter, January 1861. *Courtesy of Douglas W. Bostick.*

Castle Pinckney occupied by Southern forces. *Courtesy of Douglas W. Bostick.*

Interior of Castle Pinckney. *Courtesy of the Library of Congress.*

The Union soldiers' possession of Fort Sumter was an act of aggression that would not be resolved very quickly. A January 9 attempt by the Union ship *Star of the West* to reach Sumter with supplies ended when Citadel cadets on Morris Island fired several volleys. The ship turned and made haste for open water; these cadets would argue later that they had actually fired the first shots of the war.

Four months would pass after Anderson's initial move from Fort Moultrie. During that time, Lincoln had taken office and was faced with somewhat of a standoff. The Union president could not order Anderson to surrender because that would give credibility to the Southern cause. General Beauregard had come to Charleston to command the coastal defenses. No direct attack was at first undertaken by Beauregard, who had great regard for Anderson, one of his previous instructors at West Point. Regardless, it was widely known via rumor and printed news that a reinforcing Federal fleet was headed for Charleston, and the need for some resolution became immediate.

Though given ample opportunity to surrender his garrison, Major Anderson refused. An hour before the commencement of the Confederate attack, Colonel James Chesnut Jr. and Captain Stephen D. Lee presented Anderson with formal written notice of Beauregard's intentions. One hour later, the bombardment began.

A boat had made its way to Fort Johnson, a fortification located on the tip of James Island. There, Captain George S. James made his way to the batteries to ready them for the 4:30 a.m. opening signal. It wasn't long coming.

All eyes on Sumter. *Courtesy of Douglas W. Bostick.*

General P.G.T. Beauregard.
Courtesy of the South Carolina Historical Society.

One Charlestonian described the first shot of a war that many thought would be over in a mere week or two:

> *A sudden flash on James Island; an audible cosmic sigh from the town, lost after a moment in a deep flat report. From the mainland a spark hurtled up into the night, executing small rapid circles as it swung up and over the harbor in a wide arc, descended, seemed to hover for a split second, then burst into flame. A rending report struck the low clouds and was hurled downwards.*

Day one of the shelling found over two hundred rounds fired before Anderson responded. He had waited till sunrise to reply, saving ammunition as well. Just outside the harbor, the Union ships, under Captain Gustavus Fox, had appeared but remained distant from the action. On day two, a terrible fire broke out, and smoke billowed out and over the fort most of the day.

By the next day, Anderson was done; he surrendered to a group of Confederate officers sent to the fort representing General Beauregard. The

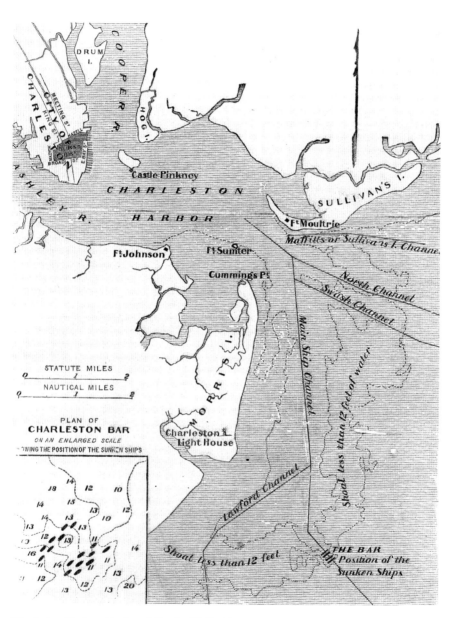

Charleston Harbor. *Courtesy of Douglas W. Bostick.*

Major General Robert Anderson. *Courtesy of Douglas W. Bostick.*

Union garrison was allowed to fire a salute to its flag before boarding one of the waiting ships, but a mishap on the parapet in preparing one of the big guns caused an explosion, killing one soldier and mortally wounding another.

One observer from a Charleston rooftop exclaimed:

> The "battle of Fort Sumter!" Good God, it wasn't a battle at all. It was little more than an exchange of civilities between gentlemen; a bloodless duel with pistols fired into the air. Commanding officers thanking God that their enemies had been spared. War was never war until men had been taught to hate.

The Civil War had begun, and it seemed that the South had fired the first shot. Charleston had become emblazoned in the minds of Northerners as the epicenter of the nation's demise, and many felt the sooner the Union regained control of Charleston, the sooner the war would end.

Seven months after the fall of Sumter, Union troops now had the upper hand, this time just seventy miles or so south of the city that had started the war. Port Royal, near Beaufort, had fallen to the Union, and Lee wasted no time heading straight to the vicinity of the attack.

CHAPTER 5

The Loss of Port Royal

Utter defeat at Port Royal. DeSaussure's and Dunovant's regiments cut to pieces. General Lee sent them they say. Preux chevalier. Booted and bridled and galant rade he. So far his bonnie face has only brought us ill luck.
—*Mary Boykin Chesnut, November 8, 1861*

The Confederacy was an amalgam of regions primarily agrarian in nature. Rice, cotton and other crops depended on the work of slaves in the field. It was affordable and effective labor that served as the cornerstone of an entire social order now on the verge of collapse.

The Federals knew the South was rich in cotton but lacked significant military industries. Once initial stocks of guns, artillery and ammunition were expended, the South's meager industrial capacity would be slow to replenish its army's needs. Out of necessity, the Confederacy would seek help from England, which, early on, seemed to sympathize with the Southern cause.

Sleek side-wheeled ships known as blockade runners would steam back and forth to England, or rendezvous in the Caribbean with English ships crammed full of guns, cannons and other military wares. Rich Southern cotton was bartered away, as if it were infinite collateral.

Medicine was also a much-needed commodity. Early casualties had not been exceptional, but both sides knew a protracted war meant much higher losses of life, with many more soldiers wounded or maimed. Again, the North led the South, with a manufacturing capacity to produce cases of laudanum, ether and surgeon's instruments. For the South, surpluses of such medicinal supplies were in short supply, and other sources would be needed. England again could help, but until then, medicines would be scavenged on the battlefield, along with food and shoes.

The Loss of Port Royal

The plan of the United States Navy was to blockade the Southern ports and destroy the flow of these much-needed supplies. Union General Winfield Scott's early proposal to Lincoln was to tactically constrict the South's troop movements and their ability to resupply. Port blockade was an important facet of what the newspapers of the day had hailed as the "Anaconda Plan." However, a base of operation was required that had a deep-water harbor; Port Royal, South Carolina, was the ideal spot.

The Confederacy never appreciated Port Royal for what it was, lacking any naval force to speak of early on during the war. The South's only concern for Port Royal was how to defend it. In May 1861, General Beauregard, together with Colonel George Elliott of Beaufort, had constructed a series of fortifications up and down the coast. From Charleston to the Savannah River, the entrances to any navigable inlet had been protected. The inherent difficulty and challenge to Beauregard was that there were so many such inlets that the enemy could compromise and thereby work its way inland.

It was everyone's guess that the Federals would cherish a base of operation from which to shut down Savannah and Charleston. General Roswell S. Ripley had approved the building of two forts at the mouth of the harbor. Ripley was an Ohio man who had married a Charleston woman and had since become a businessman and officer in the militia. He had been at the front of Charleston's defenses since going to Fort Moultrie, repairing the guns that Anderson spiked the previous December.

General Roswell S. Ripley. *Courtesy of the South Carolina Historical Society.*

Time did not permit construction of anything as massive and elaborate as Fort Sumter or Fort Pulaski in Savannah; these would be simple earthworks. Ripley and his local commander, General Thomas Drayton, were still of the mind that land-based guns trumped ship-based cannons anytime because sailed ships lacked the quick maneuverability needed to avoid the fire of land batteries.

At Bay Point, to the port's north, was Fort Beauregard, commanded by Colonel John Dunovant, who placed Captain Stephen Elliot of the Beaufort Artillery in charge of the twenty guns that were in place. To the south was Hilton Head Island, commanded by Drayton, whose brother, Captain Percival Drayton, was coincidentally assigned to Captain Samuel F. DuPont's Federal fleet. General Drayton placed Fort Walker under the immediate control of Colonel John A. Wagener and Major Arthur Huger.

Drayton and the rest of Ripley's staff knew the attack by DuPont's fleet was imminent. An informing telegram from Richmond had been sent the very day the ships set sail. Even an intervening storm at Hatteras could not deter the armada, which soon arrived off the Carolina coast only a few vessels short of its original contingent.

General Thomas W. Sherman.
Courtesy of the Library of Congress.

All together, DuPont had over seventy ships, including transports for twelve thousand soldiers under the command of Brigadier General Thomas W. Sherman. Sherman graduated from West Point, served in the Mexican War and, until recently, had been an artillery officer. He had received a letter from Winfield Scott that encouraged the army personnel to cooperate in a mission that was clearly "naval." Sherman's troops would be needed only after the harbor was in Union hands.

To promote good order and morale, Sherman issued General Order No. 13 on October 15, as the troops prepared for their journey south. He advised that no fried meats would be allowed, stating: "Soups, boiled meats and hard bread compose the true and healthy diet of the soldier on transport at sea."

The Union ships were loaded with supply wagons, ambulances, construction material and tools. Surgeon's kits, medicine, drinking water and hay for the horses rounded out the load, along with dozens of coffins, neatly stacked and secured to the bulkheads. The Confederates knew the Yankees intended to stay for a spell because Southern spies had watched as every commodity was loaded while the fleet was in the Chesapeake.

Captain Josiah Tatnall. *Courtesy of the South Carolina Historical Society.*

The only seagoing Confederate force was a small flotilla of three tugboats with only a few guns each, under the command of Commodore Josiah Tattnall, of the "Old Navy." Tattnall had fought in the War of 1812 and later chased pirates in the Caribbean. The commodore had outfitted an old river steamer with several guns to serve as his flagship. The smaller ships had the advantage of maneuverability, but they broadcast their movement and location to the enemy. Fueled by pitch pine, a thick black cloud of smoke poured out of their stacks, making them easily visible to DuPont's fleet.

Tattnall's own flagship, the *Savannah*, lulled in the mouth of Skull Creek, along with the *Resolute*, the *Lady Davis* and the *Sampson*, waiting for the enemy's advance. Then, on the morning of November 7, the attack began.

William Joseph Miller, Company H, Twelfth South Carolina Regiment, recalled the initial volleys of Federal fire, with a rather humorous concern for the nearby food supply:

> *There was a small fort with a few small cannon mounted, and plenty of sweet potato patches which were enjoyed...the Yankees sent a fleet of boats to take Beaufort, but Hilton Head was in the way. However, they soon demolished the fort...they shot bombs at us that fell in the potato patches and dug enough potatoes for several messes, but that was one time our appetites were not the trouble.*

DuPont utilized a unique strategy that soon made short work of both Southern forts. The larger Union ships sailed down the middle of the harbor, with a fleet of smaller gunboats to the starboard side. As they passed, they drew fire from the Confederate batteries, which only served to identify the location of their guns. The ships then turned south, flanking the Hilton Head position and raking it with fire. The formation then turned north and assaulted Bay Point, only to repeat the elliptical course over again.

Captain James Boatwright, Company B, Fourteenth South Carolina Regiment, McGowan's Brigade, barely survived the heavy shelling:

> *The Yankee gunboats were shelling Port Royal. He was standing in the road and saw the shell coming. Fully expecting to be killed, he turned sidewise; the shell passed him, blackening and bruising his limbs, and tearing off the skirt of his new jeans coat, the cloth of which had been woven on his mother's plantation. The shell killed four men.*

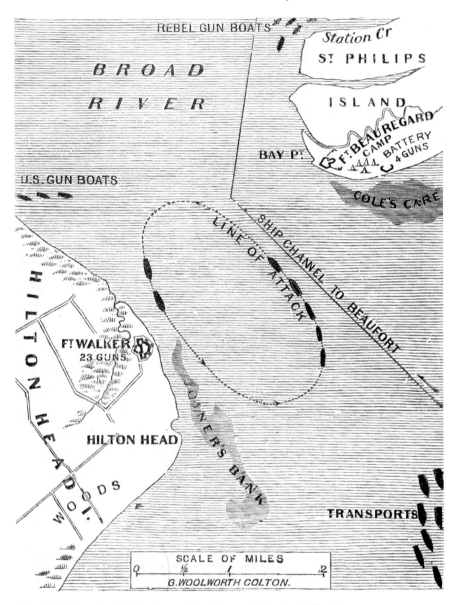

The elliptical path of DuPont's warships. *Courtesy of Douglas W. Bostick.*

The Battle of Port Royal. *Author's collection.*

Tattnall and his little navy had fully engaged DuPont's flagship, the *Wabash*, but the small Yankee gunboats soon chased the little tugs back up Skull Creek, with shells whizzing past the smokestacks and wheelhouses. The *Savannah* returned to her namesake city, with a commodore nonetheless proud of his sailor's efforts.

With just two passes, Fort Walker was done for. Guns that had been moved atop the parapets were overexposed and easily destroyed. Around two o'clock, DuPont was advised that the Confederate fort was abandoned. By nightfall, Beauregard would be evacuated as well.

The naval victory prompted General Sherman to note in his official report of November 8, 1861:

> *I deem it an imperative duty to report that the firing and maneuvering of our fleet against that of the rebels and their formidable land batteries was a masterpiece of activity and professional skills that must have elicited the applause of the rebels themselves as a tactical operation.*

General Lee arrived late at Hilton Head Island. That evening, Lee met with Ripley. The *Mercury*, one of two newspapers published in Charleston at the time, announced Lee's arrival as commander of the district. The same issue went on to touch on Ripley's reputation.

Charlestonian Emma Holmes recalled the tragedy at Port Royal in her diary entry of December 6:

> *Ripley said he would himself have commanded but, as Gen D[rayton] had planned the battles, he did not like to hurt his feelings by doing so. And Drayton assured him so solemnly that he would never leave the fort, unless as a corpse and every man killed that tears started to Ripley's eyes & he said: I will go immediately for reinforcements, every one of his aids having already been sent off. He had scarcely arrived at Hardeeville, when courier after courier galloped panting in, almost fainting from exhaustion, to say that our men had retreated. At first it was not believed, but when successive ones arrived with the same astounding news, he asked, "of course in order," but was horrified by the answer, "No, in great disorder." Gen Drayton alas fully proved his utter incompetency for his high position, but I sincerely pity him. To have been raised from an honorable position as a citizen respected by all to a distinguished military one from which he has gained nothing but contempt. However, I think the battle of Port Royal has been a great service to us, by arousing everyone from their dangerous security to the utmost vigilance & activity. The Beaufort planters will no doubt suffer greatly, but they deserve it in a great measure, for they would not remove their negroes and valuables in time, as they were long ago warned to do; as to the Yankees, the little cotton & provisions they have obtained won't pay half the expense of the expedition, and I have not the slightest doubt their dreadful treatment of the negroes, at least the men, will assuredly strengthen our "peculiar institution" by teaching them who are their true friends.*

To some members of the public and to some of his staff as well, Ripley was considered "hard to deal with":

> *Rumors of lack of cooperation between Ripley and DeSaussure—We have inquired into the matter and have authority to assert that it is entirely without foundation. On the contrary, General Ripley and General DeSaussure have acted in the most perfect unison in all arrangements in progress of the present emergency.*

Despite the *Mercury's* findings, one of Ripley's staff officers, Colonel E.M. Seabrook, acknowledged the general's "complaining." Qualifying his concern, Seabrook indicated that General Ripley usually reserved his gruffness for those who were "inept or negligent in their duties."

Ripley did not seem to fully appreciate the arrival of this supposed new commander. Lack of promotion had led Ripley to consider resigning his commission in late July. A groundswell of public support carried him until August, when he was finally promoted to brigadier general. Now, just three months later, he was placed in a situation where he felt his authority was compromised. Nevertheless, he shared in rather tentative terms what he knew of the Union success at Port Royal. For his part, Lee was cautious of Ripley, not wanting a repeat of his previous experiences in trying to coax a personality like General Loring along.

The two generals discussed what immediate resources could be put at Lee's disposal. In sum, resources of men, equipment and ammunition were scarce. Ripley then gave Lee a summation of the day's battle and reviewed various dispatches with him. The battle had quickly turned to a Federal rout of the Rebel forces.

Lee wrote to Secretary of War Judah Benjamin of his meeting with Ripley on November 9, 1861:

> *On the evening of the 7th, on my way to the entrance of Port Royal Harbor, I met General Ripley…He reported that the enemy's fleet had passed the batteries and entered the harbor….Nothing could then be done but to make arrangements to withdraw the troops…General Drayton reports he has but 955 men with him, and no field battery…Colonel Dunovant's regiment is in as destitute a condition as general Drayton's command, as they were obliged to leave everything behind, and number between 600 and 700 men.*
>
> *The enemy, having complete possession of the water and inland navigation, commands all the islands on this coast, and threatens both Savannah and Charleston, and can come in his boats within 4 miles of this place…I fear there are but few State troops ready for the field. The garrisons of the forts at Charleston and Savannah and on the coast cannot be removed from the batteries while ignorant of the designs of the enemy. I am endeavoring to bring into the field such light batteries as can be prepared.*

Confederate Colonel John A. Wagener, First Artillery, South Carolina Militia, wrote from Charleston on November 11, 1861, giving his assessment of the fight at Fort Walker:

The enemy had chosen a day that was entirely propitious to him. The water was as smooth as glass. The air was just sufficient to blow the smoke of his guns into our faces, where it would meet the column of our smoke and prevent our sight excepting by glimpses.

The sailing vessels of our opponents were towed by steamers, and thus could maneuver on the broad expanse of Port Royal with the accuracy of well trained battalions. No sooner did we obtain his range than it would be changed...while the deep water permitted him to choose his own position, and fire shot after shot.

Confederate General Drayton's report of November 24, 1861, noted ten killed in action and twenty wounded at Fort Walker. Another thirteen were wounded at Fort Beauregard.

On November 11, one of the papers in Charleston gave a laudable account of the German Artillery during the fight at Port Royal:

The German Artillery of Charleston have won for themselves the enviable distinction of having been among the chiefest participants in a battle which, for the fury and persistence of the attack, and the obstinent bravery of the defense, has no parallel in the history of this continent.

Immediately after the accolades, the grim casualty report for the German Artillery was printed, detailing the horrors of war for all to read:

Company A
Killed: Private A. Hulburg, head shot off by a ball.
Wounded: Captain D. Werner, in the mouth, 5 teeth struck out by a piece of shell.
Wounded: Private D. Semke, severely burned in the face.

Company B
Killed: Private F. Itgen, instantly by a ball.
Killed: Private W. Bringeworth, arm shot off, died in the retreat.
Wounded: Private John Klee, three fingers shot off.

On the heels of the Union naval victory, General Sherman's troops disembarked. The first order of business was the burial of the dead. The Union chaplains conducted a proper funeral service, followed by a solemn procession to the selected burial site; there were eight coffins in all. After a gun salute, each of the eight was lowered into the ground. As the dirt was

Sherman's troops land at Port Royal. *Courtesy of Douglas W. Bostick.*

Beaufort's military market. *Courtesy of Douglas W. Bostick.*

heaped upon the open graves, the emancipated Africans, lured by the site of the ceremony, began to gather around.

Thus began the mutually beneficial relationship between African and Yankee. Tired of General Sherman's prescribed rations, his men were craving fresh produce and meat. The former slaves were more than happy to oblige and, knowing their masters had fled, made repeated trips back to their plantations and returned with pigs, chickens and cattle.

Soldiers broadened the menu hunting for ducks, raccoons and deer. Information on Rebel positions was provided by contrabands eager to please their new overseers. The former slaves shared their intimate knowledge of creeks and inland trails, serving as guides.

Many of the Union troops were deeply devotional and openly prayed in groups under the moss-draped oak trees. The Africans had reoccupied the praise houses, small church structures formally used by them and their ancestors. In these confines, the sound of the "sings" drifted over the encamped Federals. Soon, the soldiers were joining in and were delighted to find that their emancipating efforts were pronounced in song. One soldier from the Fourth New Hampshire Regiment recalled the words:

Fort Walker in Union hands. *Author's collection.*

Pray on, Pray on
Pray on den light us over
Pray on Pray on
De Union Break of Day!

The force of some twelve thousand troops began to spread out through Port Royal and Beaufort, looking for any Rebel defenders who had survived the attack and scattered through the towns. Some Confederates took refuge in private homes, with the Yankees in hot pursuit.

Chance encounters between the two sides were violent and bloody. A United States marine, who fought the fleeing Rebels house to house, recalled:

I saw a Marine who was on the Wabash at the Port Royal fight. He said there were 30 men killed on his vessel. He told me also of his experience in that contest. In the first place he is not eighteen years of age. He was ordered to march at the head of a column of men 100 in number (there were two hundred two abreast), fifteen charged a house where southerners were stationed. He was ordered to go up the stairs; he saw a tall man pointing a pistol over the banister at his head. He expected to be shot but went on and got up to the head of the stairs and cut the man's throat with his cutlass. The poor fellow's pistol was not loaded, neither did he have ammunition.

The young Marine was terribly excited; a tall Irishman (on the Southern side) clubbed his musket to brain him, but it slipped to his shoulder, and the next minute the Irishman was run through the chest by the cutlass. He dreams of it now. He says he feels very bad because he killed an Irishman (he is an Irish lad). I only hope the trouble will end soon.

The reaction throughout Charleston to the loss of Port Royal was one of despair and lost hope. Many had rushed to the seawall at the peninsula's tip to hear the echoes of the cannonade, over seventy miles away. The common imagination conjured a repulse of the Union ships, a whim far from the resounding reality of defeat.

On November 9, the *Charleston Daily Courier* printed the following editorial:

The enemy has at length made the first attempt at the invasion of our state. A trifling success has been gained… To do our duty fully, let us realize the danger. To know it, is not to fear it. The more imminent it may be, the greater the effort to meet it. Let all be prepared—let every man set his hours

Charleston from the steeple of St. Michael's. *Courtesy of Douglas W. Bostick.*

in order. Let all feel that the fires and the last lesson for us in these times is to be ready at the instant to obey what they who are in command shall order.

We have to direct and lead us, brave Generals, who are accomplished soldiers and true patriots. Let not every one do what he thinks best, or wishes, it may be, without any thought whatever, but be ready to go wherever, and to do whatever, these Generals will command. Let us cast behind us fault-finding; let us come up to the work which is appointed for us, and which must be done. Let every one who can bear arms be a volunteer and ready. Ready to do whatever is required of him.

A 10:00 p.m. dispatch on November 8 from Pocotaligo, near Coosawhatchie, pinpointed the biggest dangers facing Lee's new command:

Beaufort probably will not be burned. A great deal of cotton on the islands will fall into the hands of the enemy. Bluffton will be burned if attacked...the points of danger now are: the railroad at Pocotaligo, the Charleston and Savannah.

Knowing the rail line to be a prime Yankee target, Ripley advised Lee that he intended to move Drayton's remaining force to Bluffton, while Dunovant's smaller force would be relocated to Garden's Corner. Not far from there, General Lee situated his headquarters.

The small settlement of Coosawhatchie was located in the coastal plain of southeastern South Carolina. Robert E. Lee chose to situate his headquarters there, reflecting a need to be equally accessible to Charleston and Savannah, via the railroad. It was the railroad that the Yankees needed to control in order to seize the ports by land. Lee knew this same railway was his most valuable resource, and he soon went to work organizing men and supplies for its defense.

Lee established his quarters in an abandoned house owned by Mrs. George Chisolm Mackay of Savannah. Her son, Jack, was Lee's classmate at West Point. Lee became close to the family during the winter of 1829, when Lee accepted his first engineering assignment: preparing the site for the construction of Fort Pulaski on Cockspur Island, Georgia.

The house was small and bare, save a few primitive pieces of furniture. The elegance some commanders cherished, even in the field, with silver and fine china inside a tent, was not Lee's preference. Ornamentation and "fancy things" did not concern Lee, who at times wore no insignia of rank, and who had been seen in West Virginia wearing his long coat from the "old army."

According to Gabriel E. Manigault, adjutant with the Fourth South Carolina Cavalry, Lee continued to wear his favored coat after transferring to the coast:

> *During the winter months Gen Lee occupied the little dwelling at Coosawhatchie to which he moved when he first arrived and made occasional visits to Savannah. I saw him twice then—once as he stood in the piazza of the house when I passed on horseback, and the other time when he came to the Huguenin encampment on a short visit of observation. He wore then the blue uniform of the U.S. Army with the conical shaped soft hat of the officers, the only part of his beard which was unshaven being a grey moustache. His appearance was striking and soldierly and it was impossible for him not to be noticed wherever he went.*

General Lee was frugal with his food supplies, as well. W.J. Courtney recalled an episode that exemplified his leader's habits, which set an example by the "patience and fortitude with which he bore his privations." Courtney, a veteran of the Army of Northern Virginia, told the story as follows:

> *In General Lee's tent meat is eaten but twice a week; the General, he believes the indulgence of meat to be criminal in the present straitened conditions of the country. In this connection, rather a comic story is told: having invited a number of gentlemen to dine with him, Lee, in a fit of extravagance, ordered a sumptuous repast of cabbage and middling.*

The dinner was served, and behold a great pile of cabbage, and a bit of middling about four inches long and two inches across. The guests with commendable politeness unanimously declined middling and it remained in the dish untouched. The next day the General, remembering the delicate tid-bit which had been so providentially preserved, ordered his servant to bring that middling.

The man hesitated, scratched his head and finally owned up. "De fac is, Marse Robert, dat dar middling was borrowed middling, we all didn't had nar a 'speck, an' I don paid it back to the man whard' I got it from." General Lee, heaving a sigh of deepest disappointment, pitched into his cabbage.

Having taken his last meal of the day, Lee turned to the work of war. Each night, through the late hours of darkness, Lee sat at the crude table, maps spread out, and as the candlelight flickered with the occasional breeze, he tried to imagine the enemy's next move.

CHAPTER 6

Trying to Do Much
with Little

General Lee is here, visiting the defenses. He is never hopeful and does not seem in particular good humor concerning things here. It seems to me there is miserable confusion, ignorance, and ineffeciency in every department.
—*Mary Boykin Chesnut, November 14, 1861*

The first week of November, Federal troops occupied Beaufort, South Carolina. The town's beautiful homes along the bay were soon garrisoned by Federal troops. Union Brigadier Isaac Ingalls Stevens, accompanied by the Highland Guard and the "Roundheads" of the One Hundredth Pennsylvania, found the town generally deserted. Signs of looting were everywhere, possibly the work of the recently freed slaves.

Stevens posted men about the town to prevent more theft. The town of Beaufort would have housed perhaps five hundred people during the fall and winter, being more a summer retreat for local planters. Despite Stevens's attempts to curb his own men's affection for Southern goods, their conduct was called into question, as civilians from Port Royal, Beaufort and the surrounding Sea Islands complained of theft and plunder under the guise of official action. On November 11, Union Acting Assistant Adjutant General L.H. Pelouze issued his General Order No. 24, aimed at reigning in the hoarding and looting.

Word of the enemy's transgressions traveled quickly to Lee's headquarters, but Lee was unable to respond immediately. The local forces were somewhat organized within their respective unit, but not so when combined. Lee found the overall number of recruits inadequate. Many of the soldiers were in Savannah guarding the cotton stores. Another critical issue was tenure, or length of service. State troops had been pressed into service for a period of twelve months, and soon that term would expire.

Federal troops march into Beaufort. *Courtesy of Douglas W. Bostick.*

General Stevens, seated, with his staff in Beaufort. *Courtesy of the South Carolina Historical Society.*

A letter written to Judah Benjamin from Georgia Governor Brown illustrated the frustration facing Lee and the Confederate government. Enlistments "for the war" were still few compared to the shorter state obligation.

Some governors, like Brown, seemed to feel that their control extended over troops already in the service of the New Republic. In response, on November 12, Benjamin implored Brown to see the bigger picture, for the sake of the Confederacy and that of his people:

> *There are reasons of public policy which would make it suicidal to comply with your request to withdraw Georgia troops from the enemy's front at this moment. This government will co-operate with all its power for the defense of your State, but it must do so in the manner it deems most certain to produce the desired effect of repulsing the enemy at all points, and cannot scatter its armies into fragments at the request of each governor who may be alarmed for the safety of his people. Be assured that no effort will be spared to aid you, and be good enough to communicate your confidence in this assurance to your people, thus allaying all needless panic.*

Before stationing his men in any particular area, Lee had to first survey the entire lower line of defense along the Charleston and Savannah Railroad, which at different points spanned the Combahee, Pocotaligo, Tullifinny and Coosaw Rivers. Each crossing was a precarious point where a trestle made of pine could be burned quickly to the water line, disrupting the entire rail. With the Yankees now in Beaufort, Lee spent November 9 riding up and down the lines near Pocotaligo.

Lee's focus was on the lower end of the line in Beaufort, which was closest to the enemy in Port Royal. To reinforce his efforts, Lee deployed Colonel Ambrosio José Gonzales and his siege train, consisting of several pieces of artillery mounted on railcars. Gonzales was a fiery Cuban revolutionary who had fought unsuccessfully to end Spain's domination of his island home. He came to America in the 1850s; with the onset of the Civil War, he identified with the Southern cause and offered his services.

Under Lee's direction, new fortifications were thrown up and earlier defense works were improved upon. All the while, cavalry units were deployed maintaining constant vigilance for any sign of Federal troops. The infantry was placed in strategic locations, easily mobile by way of the railroad. Much of the initial work was supervised by General Ripley, but shortly, the relationship between Ripley and Lee deteriorated to the point that Lee sent Ripley back to Charleston. Lee had suffered enough fools in

West Virginia; he would not tolerate another one here. Instead, Lee would oversee the work himself.

Lee decided to shore up both Sumter and Pulaski to withstand a sustained bombardment. After inspecting Savannah on the tenth, Lee arrived at Pulaski on the eleventh. There, he was greeted by Major Charles H. Olmstead, First Volunteer Georgia Militia. Lee directed Olmstead to reinforce the fort to the greatest extent possible to protect against Union artillery.

Being intimately familiar with Fort Pulaski, Lee cautioned that Tybee Island was less than two thousand yards away from Cockspur and that Pulaski would be in range of Union guns if Tybee was seized. Before departing, Lee ordered that the Savannah River be blocked with logjams to prevent Federal gunboats from moving upriver. Troops were to use anything available to make a nuisance for advancing Northern forces wishing to navigate toward either of the port cities.

Some good news was had on November 13, when the blockade runner *Fingal* arrived in Savannah with a large cache of arms and ammunition. The *Mercury* reprinted from the *Richmond Examiner* the full cargo list aboard:

> *12,000 Enfield Rifles, 11,000 for the Confederacy, 1,000 for Louisiana*
> *1,000,000 cartridges*
> *20 tons of powder*

Pulaski after Lee's inspection. *Courtesy of Douglas W. Bostick.*

6 24 pound rifled cannon
a quantity of sabers and a few pistols
a lot of shoes and blankets

Fraser, Trenholm and Company had negotiated quite a haul in exchange for a shipload of cotton. Captain John N. Maffitt, who as recently as November 11 had been with Lee at Coosawhatchie mapping roads and rivers, soon transferred to the command of one of the company's blockade runners.

South Carolina Governor Pickens immediately sent a telegram to Davis, notifying him of the good news. The arrival of the *Fingal* came just about the time Governor Brown was writing Secretary Benjamin demanding the return of men and arms from Virginia.

The issue of state enlistments led Benjamin to write next to General Alexander R. Lawton at Savannah, telling him to send any unarmed mustered troops to Savannah right away, but to arm only those who pledge service to the Confederate army for the duration of the war.

Benjamin's final communication of the thirteenth was to Governor Pickens, pledging to arm his troops with every gun he could spare. This support assured that Lee's forthcoming meeting with Pickens in Charleston would be a success: "As soon as I know what number of arms I have received by the *Fingal*, I will arm your troops with every musket or rifle I can possibly spare."

Governor Pickens traveled from the state capital of Columbia to Charleston in order to personally discuss with Lee their shared concerns

South Carolina Governor Pickens.
Courtesy of Douglas W. Bostick.

about enlistment terms. The foregoing matter of arming state troops led to a compromise that was agreeable to both men, with Picken's approval. South Carolina would arm half, and Lee, on behalf of the Confederacy, would arm the other half with the supplies from the blockade runner.

General Lee was further encouraged when the Southern War Department notified him that any troops currently in transit through South Carolina or Georgia would be placed at his disposal. This would help increase his troop strength considerably.

Charleston was the next city to be inspected, so the general spent November 13 through November 16 there. Up and down Meeting Street, the local militias paraded, proud to be part of the glory. Lee continued to find hesitancy among the men to volunteer for the entire term of the war. He tired of the seemingly endless routine, traveling either by train or in the saddle, with long hours and short rest. The general wrote to his daughter Mildred on November 15, describing in rather frank tones his new assignment:

> *My precious daughter: I have received your letter forwarded to Richmond by Mr. Powell, and I also got, while in the West, the letter sent by B. Turner. I can write but seldom, but your letters always give me great pleasure…I have a beautiful white beard. It is much admired. At least, much remarked on…I was unable to see your poor mother when in Richmond. Before I could get down I was sent off here. Another forlorn hope expedition. Worse than West Virginia…I have much to do in this country. I have been to*

Militia drills in front of the Citadel. *Courtesy of Douglas W. Bostick.*

Savannah and have to go again. The enemy is quiet after his conquest of
Port Royal Harbor and his whole fleet is lying there.

Lee then set out to find and place the best artillerists for service at Pulaski and Sumter, noting to General Cooper Samuel, the inspector general, on November 21, 1861:

I have the honor to report, for the information of the Secretary of War that I have just returned to this city after having inspected the batteries and posts along the coast from Charleston to Fernandina, Fla.

The guns from the less important points have been removed, and are employed in strengthening those considered of greater consequence. The entrance to Cumberland Sound and Brunswick and the water approaches to Savannah and Charleston are the only points which it is proposed to defend. At all these places there is much yet to be done, but every effort is being made to render them as strong as the nature of the positions and the means at hand will permit. They ought, after their completion, to make a good defense against any batteries that are likely to be brought against them. More guns could be usefully employed if available for this service; those at hand have been placed in the best positions and the troops distributed so as to work them to advantage. The batteries are tolerably supplied with ammunition, having about 50 rounds per gun. This amount it would be well to have increased to 100 rounds.

The greatest difficulty to be contended with is the want of artillerists and proper officers as instructors. The naval officers directed to report to me have been assigned to duty at the batteries in Charleston Harbor as ordnance and artillery officers, with the exception of Captains Buchanan and Sinclair, whom I have directed to return, having, while uncertain as to any attack being in contemplation, no appropriate duties for them to perform, and believing their services were important at their former stations.

Next, Lee found the ongoing work of blocking the streams inland to be moving slowly. It was an arduous but necessary task. The weather had been warm for November, and a few mosquitoes were in the air. But more than once alligators had caused great trepidations among the men wading in waist-deep water. One Southerner commented that he hoped the gators could wait on the Yankees; they were better fed and would make a much finer meal for the gator than any half-starved Rebel.

In front of Savannah, and at the lower end of the rail line, Lee began to oversee the construction of a deep interior line, manned with soldiers who, in this position, would be safe from the Union fleet's gunners. For almost a month, Lee's men did more work with their shovels than with their rifles.

While Lee was working near Savannah, South Carolina's governor had written to the Confederate president himself, complaining of personnel problems with certain brigadier generals and the ongoing lack of arms and ammunition. Davis replied:

> *Generals Evans and Pemberton will be sent to General Lee immediately. The deficiencies of which you speak in the character of your brigadier-generals will I hope, be compensated for by the presence of General Lee and the addition of General Pemberton.*

Davis may have already been contemplating bringing Lee back to Richmond sooner than later. Placing Pemberton along the coast with Lee gave Pemberton the time and opportunity to observe Lee's defensive strategy; a replacement for Lee was then right at hand.

Back in Savannah, Olmstead now faced a formidable threat. Federal troops moved onto Big Tybee Island on November 24, just two weeks after Lee's inspection. Hundreds of soldiers in blue worked for hours trying to place guns on the swampy island, which featured very little high ground. Once in place, the siege of Pulaski would begin.

As the Federals moved to Tybee, Captain Tatnall responded by attacking six Union vessels nearby. The commodore tried for over an hour to draw the

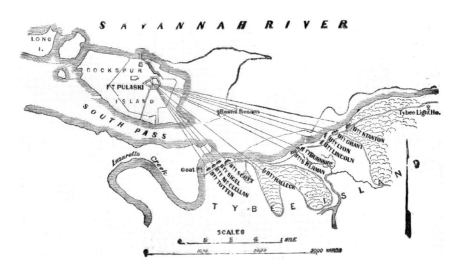

Eyes on Fort Pulaski. *Courtesy of Douglas W. Bostick.*

enemy vessels within range of Pulaski's big guns, hoping to watch as each one, in turn, was blown out of the water. The Federals wouldn't take the bait, and Tatnall withdrew, with no casualties or damage to report.

Up to this point, the North was content to dawdle in Port Royal and the surrounding area. This was, of course, fortunate for Lee because it took some time for his strategy to come together. The sudden advance to Tybee caught Lee's attention, but it caused him no great alarm. Everything that could be done at Pulaski had been done at his direction.

Lee and his staff received ongoing reports of Union transgressions; livestock was disappearing and houses were emptied of anything of value. From the small frame house that served as his base of operation, Lee wrote to his daughter Annie, sharing his concerns about the ongoing problem with Union marauders:

> *My precious Annie: I have taken the only quiet time I have been able to find on this holy day to thank you for your letter of the 29th ultimo. One of the miseries of war is that there is no Sabbath, and the current work and strife has no cessation. How can we be pardoned for all our offenses...I hope indeed that "Cedar Grove" may be saved from the ruin and pillage that other places have received at the hands of our enemies, who are pursuing the same course here as they have practiced elsewhere.*
>
> *Unfortunately, too, the numerous deep estuaries, all accessible to their ships, expose the multitude of islands to their predatory excursions, and what they leave is finished by the negroes whose masters have deserted their plantations.*

Lee then went on to note his continued frustration in getting local folks, and soldiers as well, to acknowledge the seriousness of the immediate situation: "I am trying to get a force to make headway on our defenses, but it comes in very slow. The people do not seem to realize there is a war."

On December 3, Lee wrote to Secretary Benjamin advising him of the Yankee plundering and the want of men:

> *Sir: In a letter received to-day from Col. John S. Preston, whom I had assigned to the duty of mustering into the service of the Confederate States such troops as might offer themselves for the war from the State of South Carolina or be transferred by the governor, it is stated that the only transfers made up to this time are four companies for twelve-months' service. Even for twelve months the recruiting is very languid; for the war not one company has yet offered, and not one new regiment will be organized for three months. The entire levy will be for terms less than the war, and generally for twelve months, for local defense and*

special service. I fear that there will be great delay in organizing even such a force as can be armed, unless some measures can be resorted to procure men…

I yesterday visited Port Royal sound, with the view of organizing a light force to cut off, if possible, the enemy's marauding parties on the islands. No attempts have yet been made on the main-land, nor could I discover any indication of movement. The fleet in large force lay extended across the sound from Hilton Head to Bay Point, perfectly quiescent, and no troops were visible except a picket at Hilton Head Ferry.

Benjamin knew from Lee's words that he was in a predicament. It was true irony that a new republic had been formed, with the acquiescence of the governor and people of each seceding state, yet the one key element, an army, could not be brought together.

To Lee, Benjamin responded on December 8:

I have telegraphed, announcing that measures had been taken to re-enforce you with three batteries of field artillery and three regiments of infantry, and that several other regiments would be sent. The three on the way to you are Donelson's brigade, of two Tennessee regiments, and Starke's regiment. They were all ordered to re-enforce General Floyd, but did not reach him in time to prevent his retreat. His whole force has been withdrawn from Western Virginia, and I expect further to send you Russell's Mississippi regiment, Phillip's Georgia regiment, Waddill's Louisiana battalion, and perhaps some others…I am firm in my purpose not to give a musket to a man enlisted for less than the war (or three years, which is the same thing), and therefore I beg that you will at once arm the other regiments mentioned in your letter, and if they are unable to promise troops immediately, you will please write Col. Mitchell that you are authorized by this Department to arm his regiment, and to order it to Savannah or Charleston for that purpose.

The letter carried with it a reminder of the trials and losses in West Virginia, but there was no time to dwell on the past. On December 10, Lee was preparing to leave his headquarters for a return trip to Charleston.

Lee sensed that the time was approaching when his small army would need to repel a Union advance; just where, he could not say. The railroad would move the Southern forces to the place of engagement, but coordination of such scattered forces was critical. Still, the confusion of battle, or just mere human error, could undo the best plan—that he had learned all too well at Cheat Mountain.

CHAPTER 7

Picking a Target

Have seen a copy of General T.W. Sherman's proclamation to the people of Carolina. He says he comes in a friendly spirit and does not desire to intefere with our "local institutions."
—*Mary Boykin Chesnut, December 6, 1861*

General Lee felt that, given the Union encroachment so close to Pulaski, it was time to divide his area of responsibility into districts, ensuring that there were ample commanders in the field to take immediate charge wherever the Federals chose to attack.

The first district ran from the North Carolina line to South Santee. There, Colonel A.M. Manigault commanded the Tenth South Carolina Volunteers, later famous as "Manigault's Brigade."

The second district extended from South Santee to the Stono River, near Charleston, where General Ripley was headquartered and where Lee intended for him to remain. This move greatly reduced the span of Ripley's command, but it put distance between differences of opinion.

District three was bounded by the Stono and the Ashepoo in the Colleton District. General N.G. Evans, still lauded for sensing the Federal flanking attempt at Manassas, was placed in command by Lee, with headquarters at Adams Run.

District four continued from the Ashepoo to Port Royal. General J.C. Pemberton made his camp near Lee at Coosawhatchie.

The last district was overseen by General Drayton, who worked out of Hardeeville. His forces held the remainder of the line to the Savannah River. To some, his status as a classmate of Jeff Davis at West Point shielded him from criticism over the dismal failure at Port Royal.

On December 10, Lee arrived in Charleston to conduct inspections of local defense works. The day before, Florida Governor Milton wrote a scalding letter to President Davis about the conduct of soldiers in the regular Confederate army:

> *Throughout the state the people are becoming indignant that such bodies of unarmed men and idle horses should be reared up among them, with no prospect but to consume the means of support for the women and the children, cripple the usefulness of the armed troops for defense against the enemy, and bring ruin upon the people and disgrace upon the Confederate Government.*

Lee had little knowledge of the conditions in the Federal camp at Port Royal. Nor did he have any idea that there were peculiar reasons that prevented the Union troops from mounting an offensive. Disease and disorganization were common to any army, but Union General Sherman was having a particularly bad time with both.

The same day Milton sent his letter, General Sherman wrote to General Montgomery C. Meigs in Washington, stating his dire need for a temporary hospital. Sherman went on to inform the quartermaster general that over three hundred of his men were down with malaria, and he expected the number to rise. To Sherman, it was becoming obvious that the battles with nature would have to be overcome first before taking on the Rebels.

Not that Sherman could mount an attack just yet anyway. In the same letter, he made it clear that he knew the enemy's lines and had wanted, for some time, to mount an assault but was completely without the resources to move beyond the Beaufort area.

For the most part, Sherman blamed the whole idea of combining naval and land forces for his troubles:

> *After the representations of the medical director, and my own observations as to the great number of deaths here and the continued sickness among our troops, I gave the quartermaster directions to put up a temporary hospital to accommodate 300 men. This is not a healthy climate; not near as healthy as the Potomac. The actual temperature has but little to do with it; it is the deadly malaria that arises from the swamps and the very sudden changes from hot to frosty cold. The mortality here is alarming, considering the season of the year. I have not directed any temporary barracks, and of course they will not be constructed without permission from Washington. The hospital will not cost much. It is to be single story and very temporary.*
>
> *Beaufort will answer for the sick we may have there, but it will be absolutely necessary to have one here, especially in the summer, and this*

Many mouths to feed. *Courtesy of Douglas W. Bostick*

point must be occupied, for the whole safety of the harbor depends on it and Bay Point…Our labor here is enormous. Thus far the negroes have rendered us but little assistance. Many come in and run off. They have not yet been organized to an extent we desire. The large families they bring with them make a great many useless mouths…where we get one good, able-bodied man, we have five or six women and children. They are a most prolific race.

From Charleston to Savannah, it had been generally held that the Federal landing at Port Royal constituted an invasion, a prelude to sequential attacks on one or both port cities. Certainly, Lee's urgency in building defenses and arming men was precipitated equally on that assumption.

In the same letter, however, Sherman sets forth a different mission:

In fitting out this expedition an opportunity for marching rapidly into the interior was not anticipated. The object was to seize on two important points of the coast and hold them for the protection of our blockading squadron. Therefore no more transportation was taken along than sufficient for the purposes of wood, water, and drayage for quartermaster and commissary stores, and only boats enough to assist in landing. Indeed, the number and description of boats I had nothing to do with; that was left to Captain DuPont. I have always regretted this, as we would have been far better off had we relied entirely on ourselves and not had to trust to the Navy. I am at times perfectly helpless without the Navy, and had I not depended on them,

I have not a doubt but we would have been able to land at the time of the fight, and if not assisted in reducing the work, at least have taken the whole garrison prisoners.

Captain DuPont always insisted that he would be able to and would put us ashore, but two things prevented: First the loss of all his ferry boats; and second, his failure to supply me, according to promise, with oarsmen from his ships…I never wish again, general, to co-operate. It is a thankless task…We have now a wide field before us, but we want boats, cavalry, and more force. The enemy line extends from the Ossabaw Inlet through Savannah and upon the railroad beyond Pocotaligo, and we have to choose on which point of that extended and well-garrisoned line to make a main attack, which point must depend on the amount and description of means at our disposal…

Events multiply and it is impossible to say exactly what we shall do or how we shall do it. Had I the means, I would have been on the Charleston and Savannah Railroad long ere this. Movements on water, through winding and shallow creeks, with men unaccustomed to boats, is slow, tedious, and ticklish, and I have got to see my way pretty clear now before attempting it.

"Well garrisoned" may have been over gracious on Sherman's part, at least around the first of December. Lee was just deploying his people in some orderly fashion. It is possible that Sherman said this to overstate the challenges he faced, in order to play on Meigs's sentiments. The rest of the letter speaks for itself in explaining Sherman's inability to press inland toward Lee's defenses.

By December 14, Sherman had communicated with Union General Lorenzo Thomas, the Union adjutant general, offering for his consideration a plan to attack the Southern forces. Sherman noted that the original Union plan was to have culminated in the capture of Fernandina. The recent withdrawal of the Confederate defensive line inland, as ordered by General Lee, suggested that, in fact, the Union plan had succeeded. The immediate coastline from South Edisto to Tybee was under Union control, and the deep-water port of Port Royal was operational.

Sherman saw this success as one for the United States Navy, not the army. His soldiers were bottled up along the coast, sick and demoralized. Sherman wanted another victory, but this time he wanted his men to carry the colors. Acknowledging the challenge posed by Lee's defense works, Sherman was dissuaded from considering an offensive along that front. Instead, he proposed a strategy to occupy Savannah, starting first at Pulaski.

It was there that Sherman proposed to commence the attack:

In my judgment, with the necessary means, Savannah should be the point, and to be accomplished somewhat in this way: Pulaski to be vigorously shelled, as already recommended in a former communication; at the same time the gunboats of the naval squadron to shell out the garrisons of the forts on Vernon and Augustine Rivers, to be closely followed up by the landing of the land forces in the vicinity of Montgomery and Beaulieu, thus taking Augustine River, Fort Jackson and Savannah in reverse.

I am firmly convinced that an operation of this sort would not only give us Savannah, but, if successful and strong enough to follow up the success, would shake the so-called Southern Confederacy to its very foundation.

Sherman's plan seemed to have been made regardless of the lack of equipment he had complained of earlier, disregarding the ongoing sickness in his camps, as well. The weather had not been cold enough to kill off the mosquitoes, so illnesses continued to spread. Snakes, especially water moccasins, lurked in every creek from Savannah to Charleston and beyond. This type of environment was foreign to Sherman's troops, but to Lee's men, this was home.

Sherman's idea of attacking a river crossing along the rail line was tempered by the fact that Lee had positioned men and guns at each crossing. Though these immediate forces were small, the bulk of Lee's men could be dispatched up and down the line by train, which would get them to the point of attack quicker than the Union could bring up its reserves.

General Sherman faced another problem in trying to ready his force for an offensive: he continued to suffer from a lack of laborers. Soldiers fit for duty had plenty to do with so many others out sick. Local blacks, emancipated by the presence of Federal troops, were recruited to work on various projects, such as digging ditches, extending fortifications and cleaning the camps. The Africans were now expected to work under the watchful eyes of the Union troops, whose impression of the Negroes was unfavorable. Few blacks chose to work, which prompted Sherman to make the following observations to General Thomas:

For the information of the proper authorities, and for fear lest the Government may be disappointed in the amount of labor to be gathered here from the contrabands, I have the honor to report that from the hordes of negroes left on the plantations, but about 320 have thus far come in and offered their services…The reasons for this apparent failure thus far appear to be these: 1st. They are naturally slothful and indolent, and have always been accustomed to the lash; an aid we do not make use of.

2ⁿᵈ. They appear to be so overjoyed with the change of their condition that their minds are unsettled to any plan.

3ʳᵈ. Their present ease and comfort on the plantations, as long as their provisions will last, will induce most of them to remain there until compelled to seek our lines for subsistence.

Malaria, lack of supplies and an uninspired population of former slaves continued to hold Sherman in place. While he pondered his options, a fleet of old navy ships loaded with stone was being escorted north to Charleston by DuPont's gunboats. With their harbor blocked, the people of Charleston would begin to feel the effects of the blockade. Current supplies would begin to dwindle, and food shortages and a lack of basic commodities would become reality. Sherman hoped that surrender would preclude the need for an all-out assault. Combined with the fall of Savannah, the rebellion would be squashed.

General McClellan had wired Sherman back on December 5, asking his input on how best to attack Charleston; it was December 23 before Sherman replied. General Sherman was well settled on the plan to take Savannah and had been unable, or unwilling, to confer with Captain DuPont concerning McClellan's request.

Noting that the northern portion of the Charleston peninsula had been fortified and that the Stono River had been blocked by the sinking of several vessels, it was Sherman's opinion that only a land attack could succeed:

I am inclined to the opinion that the easiest way to take or destroy the city is by the route of Sullivan's and Morris Islands, erecting batteries there, carrying Moultrie, seizing on Point Pleasant (making a demonstration by Bull's Bay if necessary) and reducing Sumter, then bringing forward the Navy and shelling the city, assisted by mortar batteries on land if necessary.

Were Charleston and Savannah to fall, the Confederacy would then have only the ports of Wilmington and New Orleans. Without knowing the contents of any of the Union dispatches, General Lee had long understood the urgency of keeping both cities safe and operational. He knew that Charleston was by far the more sentimental target for the Yankees, but Lee remained tentative about Savannah's fate, as well.

Returning to Charleston on December 11, Lee left behind a variety of projects that would be supervised by his field commanders. One problem that had come to Lee's attention was sickness in his own camps. Recalling the pitiful condition of so many of his men in western Virginia, Lee directed his assistant adjutant, Colonel Taylor, to issue General Order No. 4, concerning sanitation. Personal hygiene, camp cleanliness and exposure to the sun were all sited as techniques to avoid disease.

Typhoid fever ran through some of Lee's regiments, and the burden of caring for the soldiers fell to the civilians. One of Lee's men recalled the kind treatment he received in Colleton District, between Charleston and Beaufort:

> *Captain Miller got me in a private home, there being no hospitals at this place (Green Pond, S.C.). The name of the family was Harrison, very wealthy people…they were very kind and nice to me. Mr. Randolph Pierce was detailed nurse for me. I was there a month. After getting so I could eat, one of the girls came to me and asked me if I could eat boiled custard, and I, of course said "yes-mam." She brought in a glass, also a spoon. That was the first time I had seen that kind of custard. They had not gotten to boiling custards in the up country at that time.*

Lee had no idea that on the evening of December 11, he would witness the destruction of fully a third of the city hated most by the North for inciting the rebellion. Ironically, the Yankees would have nothing to do with the disaster.

"Old Sesh," *Harper's Weekly*, December 14, 1861. "A Short Blanket: While I cover my Neck, I expose my Feet, and if I cover my Feet, I expose my Neck. Ugh!" *Courtesy of Douglas W. Bostick.*

CHAPTER 8

Smoke and Stones

Carolina institute, where secession was signed, burned down. From East Bay, along Broad St. down to the river—Mr. Petigru's house. So being anti secession does not save. The fire, as the rain, falls on the just and the unjust.
—Mary Boykin Chesnut, December 14, 1861

Lee and members of his staff had arrived at Charleston from Coosawhatchie, crossing over the Ashley River by rowboat. The aura of a fire was plain for all to see, but it was way over on the opposite side of the peninsula city. Mrs. C.E. Chichester was quartered at Castle Pinckney with her husband, who was commander of the Charleston Zouave Cadets. During this period of time, Castle Pinckney was a prisoner-of-war camp, where over one hundred Yankees captured at Manassas were housed. Chichester recalled the outbreak of the fire:

> *It commenced about 8 o'clock in the night…there was a slight wind blowing from the north-east, it spread slowly, as the tide rose, the wind increased and the fire spread rapidly…it soon passed beyond the control of the firemen who had only the old hand engines and wells and cisterns to aid them…Furniture and bedding was carried out into the wide streets, squares and vacant lots, little children and sick ones placed on the bedding, which soon took fire from the sparks falling all around, and the children had to be rescued, some by a stranger…At the Castle, the fire was soon observed by the sentinels, and the entire garrison watched it anxiously…my husband made a detail of as many men as the post boat could possibly carry and sent them over to the city to render what assistance they could…I was lying in bed suffering from a most excruciating headache…my colored maid, the*

man cook and the waiting man were in the next room where they could see and note the progress of the fire…truly it was a fearful night.

Thinking little of the fire at first, General Lee and his entourage arrived at the Mills House Hotel on Meeting Street for dinner. Afterward, Lee retired to the parlor to chat with his staff officers, including Taylor and Captain Joseph C. Ives. Not long afterward, Lee and the others became aware of the growing sense of alarm. It was suggested that a view from the hotel roof would give the best indication of the progress of the fire.

All around him, Lee beheld a spectacle of destruction. A gusty wind was blowing cinders and ash everywhere, and it was obvious that the fire was only a block or so away. Rushing back downstairs, the men found ladies and babies ready for evacuation. One of the staff officers went out the front, only to be repulsed by the intense heat. Lee accompanied his party down to the basement and outside by way of the rear staircase. The group then got into several carriages and made the trip to High Battery, where the home of Mr. Charles Alston was placed at their disposal by his son. As his parents were out of town, young Mr. Alston made every attempt to ensure everyone's comfort and safety.

To the rescue, 1861. *Author's collection.*

The diary of Charleston's Miss Emma Holmes recalled: "Hour after hour of anxiety passed, while flames raged more fiercely and the heavens illuminated as if it were an aurora borealis—it was terrifically beautiful."

The fire, likely the worst the city had ever seen, started on the east side in the vicinity of Hassell Street and East Bay, amongst the trash and refuse generated by a sash and blind factory. This was the fire's location when first observed by Lee and his officers from their rowboats. The fire then spread toward the west and southwest, engulfing everything in its path. Soon the Circular Congregational Church on Meeting Street was ruined. Eventually, General Ripley ordered groups of houses to be blown up to stop the surge of flames. President Lincoln may have smiled if he knew that the fire destroyed St. Andrews Hall, where the Ordinance of Secession was debated, and Institute Hall, where the document of the rebellion was signed into effect.

There is no historical record that Ripley and Lee were together at any time that night, and given their tepid relationship, it is probably for the better. Lee was not one to shirk responsibility. Likely, he saw Ripley's success in coordinating men and material. Lee knew, too, that Ripley lived in the city and had intimate knowledge of the streets and neighborhoods. Thus, Ripley knew just where to place the gunpowder to stem the flaming tide, receiving accolades for his work during the catastrophe.

On December 12, the *Mercury* newspaper wrote:

> *The energy and firmness displayed by Gen. Ripley during the fearful scenes of Wednesday night, have justly won for him the gratitude and respect of our whole community. Riding, as he constantly was, in the very teeth of the fire, his coolness, vigilance and intrepidity were conspicuous, as we know they would be upon the field of battle. Certain it is that nothing but his prompt*

Charleston after the fire of 1861. *Courtesy of Douglas W. Bostick.*

assumption of the responsibility of blowing up the intervening buildings could ever have saved the Catholic Orphan Asylum, the Roper Hospital (containing hundreds of sick) and the houses beyond that structure.

Having avoided personal loss or injury in the fire, General Lee turned to the formidable tasks that lay ahead. On December 16, Lee wrote to Secretary Benjamin about the results of his inspections around Charleston:

The island defenses around the city, commencing on the coast side of James Island, extending to Wappoo Creek, thence to Ashley River, across the neck between Ashley and Cooper, and from the branch through Christ Church Parish to the sound, are in good state of progress, and will now give steadiness and security to our troops in any advance of the enemy from any of those quarters, and afford time to move troops to meet them. The works have been mostly constructed by labor furnished by the planters. I hope they will be complete this week. The batteries in the harbor are in good condition, and if properly served should arrest the approach by the channel. Wappoo Creek is also provided with batteries in addition to those previously constructed at the mouth of the Stono, which should stop vessels by that direction. They form part of the land defense and points of support where they touch the creek.

Lee then continued his inspections of local fortifications. Mrs. Chichester observed General Lee as he inspected Castle Pinckney, the third Charleston fort checked personally by him for troop strength, gun placement and ammunition:

He made a very minute examination of every department and before leaving, remarked that he found the Castle in better condition, in every respect than any of the other forts, and complimented the garrison on its fine military appearance, and the order and discipline which prevailed in every department.

Soon, six more thirty-two-pounders, three eight-inch Columbiads and one twenty-four-pound siege gun were en route to Charleston. Lee prayed that all his earthworks and batteries would be completed before the Union troops began their offensive. Could he have known the difficulties Sherman faced at Port Royal, Lee would have perhaps slowed his pace. Not knowing this, Lee pressed ahead, mindful that time was of the essence for his work along the entire lower Confederate coastline.

ALL IN A DAY'S WORK

Young men of privilege in the South were dependent on slave labor for the tough tasks and did not come into the war with calloused hands and sturdy backs. One such recruit, August Dickert, describes his tribulations:

My first duty as a soldier, I will never forget. I went with a detail to Steven's Iron Battery to build embrasures for the forts there. This was done by filling cotton bags the size of 50-pound flour sacks with sand, placing them one upon the top of the other at the opening where the mouths of cannons projected, to prevent the loose earth from falling down and filling in the openings. The sand was first put upon common wheel-barrows and rolled up single planks in a zig-zag way to the top of the fort, then placed in the sacks and laid in position. My turn came to use the barrow, while a comrade used the shovel for filling up. I had never worked a wheel-barrow in my life, and like most of my companions, had done but little work of any kind. But up I went the narrow zig-zag gangway, with a heavy loaded barrow of loose sand. I made the first plank all right, and the second, but when I undertook to reach the third plank on the angles, and about fifteen feet from the ground, my barrow rolled off, and down came sand, barrow, and myself to the ground below.

I could have cried with shame and mortification, for my misfortune created much merriment for the good natured workers. But it mortified me to death to think I was not man enough to fill a soldier's place. My good co-worker and brother soldier exchanged the shovel for the barrow with me, and then began the first day's work I had ever done of that kind…but I was not by myself; there were many others as tender as myself. Young men with wealthy parents, school and college boys, clerks and men of leisure, some who had never done a lick of manual labor in their lives, and would not have used a spade or shovel for any consideration, would have scoffed at the idea of doing the laborious work of men, were now toiling away with the farmer boys, the overseers' sons, the mechanics—all with a will—and filled with enthusiasm that nothing short of the most disinterested patriotism could have endured.

Wheelbarrows, picks and shovels. *Courtesy of Douglas W. Bostick.*

Whether through divine intervention or just fate, as Lee shored up his defenses, Union General Sherman opined to General McClellan the loss of opportunity and the lack of resources. On December 19, Sherman wrote:

I have received your kind letter of the 5th, and hasten to say that I think that the trip to Fernandina is lost for the present. I have been in readiness for some time, keeping all the vessels destined thither waiting for the Navy to be ready, but have found that the latter has a new job on its hands, viz, the convoying and sinking the vessels of the stone fleet; also, for reasons already given in an official letter, I believe the public interest will be much advanced by deferring it now—it has been postponed so long. It was unfortunate that the naval fleet had to send for more ammunition after the affair of Port Royal, as Fernandina would have been taken then without much trouble, and no doubt it could be easily taken now; but it has been re-enforced and fresh artillery sent there. It has a garrison of about 1,300 men and four forts, one of which is on Cumberland Island. Fort Clinch, though never yet finished, has a partial armament. We have understood that Brunswick has quite a large garrison, but cannot find out any particulars.

Commodore DuPont thinks he will be ready for Fernandina in a week or two, but I am inclined to believe that the wants of Tybee and Saint Helena will divide him too much until those places are made perfectly safe... Tattnall is busy reconnoitering with his fleet, and Pulaski has been filled with men during the past few days...I have opened the passage around Port Royal Island, which the enemy attempted to close, but their batteries fired into our boat and hit her once, doing no damage.

As it will be some time before proper preparations can be made for Savannah, I am inclined towards seizing upon the south end of the Charleston and Savannah Railroad, as soon as I can get the cavalry. To do this I must be sure of success, for it is quite a vital point in our success on Savannah. I think it can be done at a dash, properly executed, but then the security of our communications will have to be looked to against forays from Coosawhatchie, a point on the railroad strongly fortified. I have tried to get this railroad destroyed, but thus far without success, though our party has not returned.

The stone fleet.
Courtesy of Douglas W. Bostick.

As to the point of Charleston, of which you desire me to speak, I will have pleasure of writing you in a day or two. If we are to operate inward, I think another light battery here very necessary, as well as a regiment of cavalry and infantry, as stated in my official communication.

On December 20, the one-year anniversary of the secession of South Carolina from the Union, the stone fleet from Port Royal arrived at the mouth of Charleston Harbor. The old ships were scuttled, partially blocking the harbor entrance. As if Lee's resolve needed any affirmation, the actions of the Union forces incensed him. Charleston's women and children, the old and infirm, depended on the supplies brought in by the blockade runners for their survival. To Lee, this was yet more evidence of a conflict lacking any sense of morality. In fact, the *Mercury* printed its response to the harbor obstructions, calling the Union "mad with folly and revenge."

Deciding the enemy's lack of civility was an omen, Lee wrote to Secretary Benjamin on the evening of the twentieth:

This achievement, so unworthy any nation, is the abortive expression of the malice and revenge of a people which it wishes to perpetuate by rendering more memorable a day hateful in their calendar. It is also indicative of their despair of ever capturing a city they design to ruin, for they can never expect to possess what they labor so hard to reduce to a condition not to be enjoyed. I think, therefore, it is certain that an attack on the city of Charleston is not contemplated, and we must endeavor to be prepared against assaults elsewhere on the south coast.

Having returned to Coosawhatchie, Lee wrote to Andrew G. Magrath of Charleston on the eve of the state convention about his concerns for the Southern cause. Magrath was the former federal judge in Charleston who discarded his robes in the courtroom upon learning of Charleston's secession. Magrath had solicited Lee's input concerning state troops joining Confederate service:

I tremble to think of the consequences that may befall us next spring when all our twelve month men may claim their discharge, at the beginning of the campaign, when our enemies will take the field fresh and vigorous, after a year's preparation and winter repose, we shall be in all the anxiety, excitement and organization of new armies.

In what different condition will be the opposing armies on the plains of Manassas at the resumption of active operations. I have thought that

Judge Andrew MacGrath. *Courtesy of Douglas W. Bostick.*

General George B. McClellan was waiting to seize the advantage he would then possess. I beg you will put a stop to this lamentable state of affairs.

The Confederate States have now but one great objective in view, the successful issue of their war of independence. Everything worth their possessing depends on that. Everything should yield to its accomplishment.

Christmas Day 1861 dawned without any immediate threats to Lee's line. The general was able to spend the day giving small gifts to his officers' children and to his servants. A good deal of time was spent writing to family. To his wife, Lee wrote of his hope for an end to the conflict. He considered the future, dismissing talk of England's intervention on the side of the Confederates. At length, he mused over the condition of his homeland and his plans once the fighting subsided.

Ever true to his austerity of body and soul, Lee talked of a humble homestead, with humble meals:

I cannot let this day of grateful rejoicing pass, dear Mary, without some communication with you. I am thankful for the many among the past that I

Stratford, Lee's boyhood home. *Courtesy of Douglas W. Bostick.*

have passed with you and the remembrance of them fills me with pleasure. For those on which we have been separated we must not repine. If it will make us more resigned and better prepared for what is in store for us, we should rejoice. Now we must be content with the many blessings we receive. If we can only become sensible of our transgressions, so as to be fully penitent, and forgiven, that this heavy punishment under which we labour may with justice be removed from us and the whole nation, what a gracious consummation of all that we have endured it will be!

I hope you had a pleasant visit to Richmond…If you were to see this place, I think you would have it, too. I am here but little myself. The days I am not here I visit some point exposed to the enemy, and after dinner at early candle-light, am engaged in writing till eleven or twelve o'clock at night… As to our old home, if not destroyed, it will be difficult ever to be recognized. Even if the enemy had wished to preserve it, it would almost have been impossible. With the number of troops camped around it, the change of officers etc., the want of fuel, shelter, etc., and all the dire necessities of war, it is vain to think of its being in a habitable condition. I fear too, books, furniture, and the relics of Mount Vernon will be gone. It is better to make up our minds to a general loss. They cannot take away the remembrance of the spot, and the memories of those that to us rendered it sacred. That will remain to us as long as life will last, and that we can preserve.

In the absence of a home, I wish to purchase "Stratford." That is the only other place that I could go to, now accessible to us, that would inspire me with feelings of pleasure and local love. You and the girls could remain there in quiet. It is a poor place, but we could make enough corn-bread and bacon for our support, and the girls could weave us clothes. I wonder if it is for sale and at how much. Ask Fitzhugh to try to find out, when he gets to Fredericksburg. You must not build your hopes on peace on account of the United States going into a war with England. She will be very loath to do that, notwithstanding the bluster of the Northern newspapers. Her rulers are not entirely mad…

We must make up our minds to fight our battles and win our independence alone. No one will help us. We require no extraneous aid, if true to ourselves. But we must be patient. It is not a light achievement and cannot be accomplished at once…I wrote a few days since, giving you all the news, and have now therefore nothing to relate. The enemy is still quiet and increasing in strength. We grow in size slowly but are working hard. I have had a day of labour instead of rest, and have written at intervals to some of the children. I hope they are with you, and inclose my letters.

Lee's Christmas presents came in the form of dispatches received throughout the day. Secretary Benjamin wired confirmation of the promised shipment of artillery. General Ripley wrote, giving a summary of troops available throughout the second military district, and reported on the progress of the defense works. He was proud to report that the lines on James Island were working toward completion. Regrettably, Colonel Manigault of the first military district reported the loss of a blockade runner loaded with salt and fruit, noting that all the cargo was lost when the ship burned.

On December 27, Lee generated several dispatches. He wrote to Governor Pickens, in reply to his concerns about the organization of certain units in the field. In sobering terms, Lee set forth the reality of the moment:

The enemy is making demonstrations against Wadmalaw Island, and our force there is not strong enough to resist him. Since your letter authorizing me to take command of the State troops in the field, I have felt no hesitation in doing so. Previously, although aware that certain forces were called into service and placed under the command of General Ripley, I did not know when or how it was designed to use them. According to the last returns received the number of troops mustered in Confederate Service from South Carolina within the department present for duty is 10,036 including officers, non-commissioned officers, and privates.

My objective is to inform your excellency of the amount of the force for actual service in the state. You must, however, bear in mind that the garrisons for the forts at Georgetown, of Fort Moultrie, Forts Sumter, Johnson, Castle Pinckney, and the field works for the defense of the approaches through Stono, Wappoo ,etc. which embrace the best and steadiest of our troops, cannot be removed from their posts, and must not therefore be included in the force for operations in the field.

The strength of the enemy, as far as I am able to judge, exceeds the whole force that we have in the state. It can be thrown with great celerity against any point, and far outnumbers any force we can bring against it in the field.

Next, Lee wrote to General Ripley, trying to distinguish what units were "twelve month" and which ones were "for the war." Only the latter would be armed with the precious Enfield rifles. Muskets, shotguns, handguns and even bowie knives would make up the armaments of the short-timers:

Please inform me whether Maj. Edward Manigault's battalion has entered the Confederate service for twelve months or for the war. If for the latter period, it might be united with Lieutenant-Colonel Moore's battalion, and by the addition of the two companies reported by Colonel Preston to have been mustered in for the war by him would form a regiment for the war…All the companies could then be armed with the Enfield rifles by Colonel Preston, and placed under the command of Col. Carter L. Stevenson (Formally of the old service), or such other officer as the President might think proper.

This same day, the twenty-seventh of December, Colonel Manigault reported to Assistant Adjutant Washington, giving his overview of the first military district:

A great portion of my force here, consisting of 650 men of Harlee's Legion will…be disbanded within a week…as the measles and mumps have broken out…with the long line of coast to be watched and guarded, the force that will be left me on the 1st of January will scarcely be adequate. I am aware that there are other more exposed and more important districts, requiring all the available force for its defense, and it may not be possible to re-enforce me. I do, however, desire to know of what my means of defense consist, so that more may not be expected of me than my force would warrant.

Colonel C.J. Elford of the Sixteenth Regiment, South Carolina Volunteers, had informed General Ripley just the day before that his men were as good as naked before the enemy:

Lee's men guard the ferry crossing. *Courtesy of Douglas W. Bostick.*

> *I have the honor to report that my regiment is not in a position to move with efficiency immediately. One of our companies is unarmed. Of the remaining arms, about 100 have proved defective and are in the hands of the armorer for repair. We have not a bayonet-belt, or scabbard, or cartridge-box in the regiment. Major Eason, the ordnance officer, informed me to-day that these would be procured in eight or ten days. We have about three rounds of cartridges and caps, but I understand that ammunition can be obtained. I have been pressing our requisition for accouterments continually since we have been here, but hitherto without success. So soon as we can procure these we are ready and anxious to march to the point of duty.*

The only attempt by the Union to break out of Port Royal came late on the night of December 31, 1861, when Federal General Stevens's brigade, together with soldiers from the Forty-eighth New York, the Forty-seventh and Fiftieth Pennsylvania and some New Hampshire volunteers, mounted a fleet of flatboats that coursed effortlessly over the river obstructions Lee had put in place.

The engagement occurred in the district commanded by Pemberton. At the oars were former slaves eager to please their new benefactors. Led by their gunboats, the Union's plan was to attack the Port Royal Ferry Station at Seabrook Landing, thus opening Coosaw Creek to Federal control. Stevens had also loaded two navy howitzers for support. The Confederate position was well supported, but eventually the Rebels withdrew with cavalry guarding their rear. General Stevens recalled the skirmish, which was briefly, but hotly, contested:

The column had advanced a mile in this order when a puff of smoke and the roar of a gun burst from the edge of the woods, followed by others in rapid succession, and a battery, well screened in the timber, opened a rapid fire of shells over and among the leading regiments…until the third regiment, the Michiganders, was fully abreast with the battery. Then halting, he brought his three leading regiments into line, facing the woods, wheeling them to the right, and advancing the Highlanders and 50th on a line with the Michiganders, and threw out four companies of the latter upon the battery.

The Michigan skirmishers had scarcely disappeared within the bushes which masked the battery, when a rolling volley of musketry rattled among the trees, and out they came, falling back. At the same time a large regiment of the enemy appeared from behind a point of the woods which partially screened its advance, bearing directly down upon the 50th Pennsylvania. Colonel Christ was directed to meet and not to await the attack. At the command his regiment deliberately fixed bayonets and moved forward,

Attack at Port Royal Ferry. *Courtesy of Douglas W. Bostick.*

presenting a long and imposing line. The charging rebel regiment first ceased its shouts and yells, then fired a scattering and ineffective volley, and broke and fled to the cover of the woods so precipitantly that the 50ᵗʰ had scarcely time to fire a round after them…the hostile battery ceased its fire, and the troops, on reaching its position, found the enemy gone, with every sign of a precipitate retreat…the substantial confederate earthworks were reduced, and the troops returned to Hilton Head.

Lee wrote to his son Custis on January 4 about the Yankee advance:

Enemy quiet & retired to his islands. The main (land) seemed too insecure for him & he never went 400 yards from his steamers, not even to the extent of the range of his guns. After burning some houses on the river bank, and feeling our proximity unpleasant, he retreated to Port Royal again. I hope we may always be able to keep him close. But he can move with great facility and rapidity and land where he can bring his steamers and burn, pillage and destroy, and we cannot prevent him.

Had General Stevens had his way earlier, Lee may not have had time to prepare. The attack of January 1 was planned some time before, but it failed to get General Sherman's approval at the time because of a lack of manpower, cavalry and the many other concerns Sherman shared with General Meigs:

Immediately after landing (at Hilton Head), General Sherman held a conference with his general officers as to undertaking an offensive movement. The enemy was evidently demoralized, and either Charleston or Savannah might fall before a sudden dash, and offered a tempting prize. But the general opinion was that movement upon either involved too great risks, and that the first duty was to fortify and render absolutely secure the point already gained.

General Stevens alone dissented from this view. He strenuously urged an aggressive movement inland to the mainland, then, turning to right or left, against one of the cities. In answer to objections, he declared that the overpowering naval force rendered Hilton Head already secure, and it could be fortified at leisure. The navy, too, could support an advance, and cover a withdrawal in case of need.

The country was full of flatboats used by the planters for the transportation of cotton. Hundreds of these could be collected among the islands by the Negroes, and would furnish means of transporting the troops up, or ferrying them across the inland waters, which instead of an obstacle, could thus be made an aid to the movement. But the cautious counsel prevailed.

Fate chose to side with the Confederacy, and Lee had time to prepare. Had Sherman been more aggressive, heeding Stevens's suggestions, Charleston, and perhaps Savannah as well, would have easily fallen to the North. With that, Union control of the Charleston and Savannah Railroad would have been guaranteed. On the heels of the misfortunes at Cheat Mountain, Lee's abilities would have again been called into question.

Mercifully, the first year of the war had ended. The victory at Manassas was a distant echo of a cause now faltering and struggling for survival. The Richmond government was despised by many of the Confederate governors, who squabbled over every soldier and every gun. Throughout his command, Lee was losing hundreds of state volunteers that Davis and Lee hoped would join the Confederate army.

The conflicts between both political and military personalities, the shortages of supplies and, most of all, the sickness all ran together in Lee's mind as one big reminder of a time and place not long ago. This had indeed been a bad year for Lee, and nothing around him suggested that things would be any better in the year to come. Still, he had much to be thankful for. Lee's family had so far endured the conflict, but his separation from them caused him much anxiety.

The defense line protecting the Charleston and Savannah Railroad had done its job of deterring the Yankees from attack, but Stevens's New Year's surprise served to put the Southern forces on higher alert. By now, the stones dumped in the channel were scattered by the current, but they still reminded Lee that the North would stop at nothing to win. Lee now sensed that Savannah, not Charleston, would be the center point of any forthcoming enemy initiative. The general felt a relocation of his headquarters to that city would be prudent.

CHAPTER 9

Reconciliation

For the enemy is exultant and bent upon our destruction. We are a rattlesnake confederacy. We have taught him to think twice before they move. No rash advances now—followed by the first sprightly running of Bull Run.
—*Mary Boykin Chesnut, February 11, 1862*

Lee began the second year of the war much as he had finished the last. Each day, there were new units to organize, equipment to distribute and defense works to be improved. For Lee, there was never enough of anything, and the reaction of the troops to building defenses resulted in a new nickname: "King of Spades."

Lee had received a letter from Governor Pickens on December 31, voicing concern over the appointment of General Beauregard's son to officer's rank. The appointment seemed to have created some bad feelings with some of Ripley's men, who felt they were more deserving of the promotion. On January 7, Pickens wrote to President Davis on the matter:

I do not know if it prevails elsewhere in the Army, but I take the liberty to inform you that I fear the feeling of General Ripley towards General Lee may do injury to public service. His habit is to say extreme things even before junior officers, and this is well calculated to do great injury to General Lee's command. I do not think General Ripley means half what he says in his energetic way, but others construe it differently.

From a copy of the report of forces sent to General Lee by General Ripley, up to December 1, I find many very important omissions. I suppose it must be from inadvertence, for I do not think Ripley at all exact in relation to the infantry I have sent General Lee a correct return. General Lee is a perfect head, quiet and retiring. His reserve is construed disadvantageously. I find him all that a gentleman should be, and all that ought to be expected of a thorough and scientific officer. The two are in contrast.

During this time, Lee chose to take the high road and ignore Ripley's assertions. Instead, he turned to what concerned him the most. During the winter, Federal troops had scouted Lee's positions, explored the vast network of rivers, sounded the channels and mapped the terrain. For his part, General Sherman kept up his initiative, preparing for an offensive and considering every option. Still, Lee's defense works plagued him. Sherman knew the railroad had to be compromised, and after deliberating with his staff, he returned to his first preference for engagement: Savannah.

On January 8, Lee wrote to General Samuel Cooper, his adjutant and inspector general, tempering any optimism expressed recently in the newspapers:

From a paragraph in the Charleston and Savannah journals, to which my attention has been called, I fear I may have inadvertently misled the Department as to my opinion of the strength of the defenses of those cities and of my ability to prevent the enemy from penetrating into the interior of the country. In my letters describing the works and batteries in progress of construction, to which I cannot now refer, I intended to express the hope rather than the confident assurance that when completed, armed and manned, if properly fought, the enemy's approach ought to be successfully resisted.

Lee then continued to give his thoughts on the enemy's intentions:

I have thought his purpose would be to seize upon the Charleston and Savannah Railroad near the head of Broad River, sever the line of communication between those cities with one of his columns of land troops, and with his other two and his fleet by water envelope alternately each of those cities. This would be a difficult combination for us successfully to resist.

General Lee's speculations now ran parallel with General Sherman's hopeful plan of action. It began to appear that, at a distance, a magnificent game of blind chess was emerging, wherein neither player knew the other's exact move and the winner would only know he had won when the other player lost.

Reconciliation

During the second week in January, Lee visited the Confederate defense works at Fernandina, Cumberland and Brunswick. There he found that many more heavy guns were needed. Cannon powder was in short supply, and at Amelia Island, the Rebels were without accoutrements, shoes and ammunition. Fort Clinch was doing good duty by itself: its imposing inner and outer walls proved safe haven for many blockade runners and their precious cargo.

Returning from his Florida inspections, Lee stopped at Cumberland Island. It was here that his father, the Revolutionary War hero Henry Lee III, was buried on March 15, 1818. While serving under General Nathanael Greene, Harry had become famous chasing Cornwallis out of the Carolinas, earning the moniker "Light Horse Harry."

In death, Harry Lee's continence had faded to that of an irresponsible gambler of fortune. His dashing heroics in the war against Britain were now far-off memories of a war fought long ago. Torn between the life of an army officer and that of a business speculator and trader, Lee chose the latter, abruptly resigning his army commission. To many who knew him, Harry Lee simply gave up, or gave in to an out-of-control compulsion. Opposed to another war with Great Britain, Harry had come to the aid of newspaper

"Light Horse Harry" Lee. *Courtesy of the South Carolina Historical Society.*

Grave of "Light Horse" Harry Lee. *Courtesy of M. Kirkley Ferguson.*

editor Alexander Hanson, whose home was attacked by a mob bent on destroying him and his antiwar paper. Taken from a jail that proved to be a false haven, at least one person was killed, and Harry was beaten, cut and mutilated. Shame, both public and private, had followed him eventually to Barbados, where he was safe from debtor's prison and ridicule.

Sick and longing for home, Lee attempted a return to Virginia. His deteriorating condition caused him to be landed at Cumberland Island, off the South Georgia coast. At Dungeness, the island compound that had been the property of General Greene, Harry attempted to mend his health, nursed by Greene's daughter. He died shortly thereafter.

General Lee had not seen his father since he was a small child of six, when Harry first left for the Caribbean. He, with the rest of the family, had heard the stories and rumors, which served only to dishonor the Lee family name. Lee had never visited this final resting place, even though his assignment at Cockspur Island in 1829 brought him close by. Mourning the loss of his beloved mother on July 10 of that year may have made a trip to the cemetery too foreboding.

While assigned at Cockspur as a second lieutenant of engineers, Lee frequented the Savannah home of Jack Mackay, his academy classmate. Smitten by one of Jack's sisters, Lee's eventual transfer order to Fort Monroe, Georgia, brought the budding romance to a close.

Subsequently, the public exposure surrounding General Lee's half brother, Henry Lee, compounded the tarnish upon the Lee family name. An affair with his wife's sister would cost Henry his appointment as consul to Morocco. With the Lee family's legacy diminished, marriage into the honorable family of Eliza Mackey was out of the question.

Now, thirty-three years later, a visit to his father's grave site was more acceptable to Lee. The black mark on the Lee name had faded, and though General Lee's efforts had not yet gained fame, he had done nothing to shame his family's honor. Lee perhaps found hope in his determination not to follow in his father's path. Writing to his wife, he noted the visit:

While at Fernandina I went over to Cumberland Island and walked up to Dungeness, the former residence of General Green. It was my first visit to the house and I had the gratification at length of visiting my father's grave. He died there, you may recollect, on his way from the West Indies, and was interred in one corner of the family cemetery. The spot is marked by a plain marble slab, with his name age and date of his death…the garden was beautiful, enclosed by the finest hedge I have ever seen. It was of the wild olive.

General Lee wrote to Custis on January 19, 1862, about the trip and about the current status of the enemy: "I was at Dungeness. The garden was beautiful. He is quiescent still. What he is preparing for or where he will strike I cannot discover."

Inspired by the visit to Cumberland Island, Lee began a methodic study of the enemy, looking for any activity that would betray their intentions. Lee did not have to look far; on January 25, another stone fleet was sunk in Charleston.

Lee then received reports that the Federals were clearing the river obstructions at Walls Cut on the inland waterway. This was a critical area because it was here that Port Royal was linked to the Savannah River. Union General Sherman wrote to Simon Cameron, the United States secretary of war, on January 7:

> From letters above referred to it may be seen that if we attack Savannah on both sides a very large force will be requisite. I think the force should be sent so that we can not only meet any emergency and attack in the manner that circumstances will prove to be the best, but so that we can have force large enough to follow up rapidly our success.
>
> I am trying to open up Wall's cut, and if successful, the Navy, I think, will be able to throw gunboats into Savannah River, and we to erect batteries on some of its islands, cut off Fort Pulaski, shell Fort Jackson, and afterwards, the city, without the slow and expensive process of first bombarding Pulaski.

The enemy's actions had confirmed Lee's suspicions. On February 3, Lee moved his headquarters to Savannah. Elsewhere, Union troops were advancing toward Paducah, Kentucky, while a Federal fleet of gunboats began making its way toward Confederate Fort Henry.

CHAPTER 10

A Confederacy in Crisis

Awful news today. Ft. Donelson a drawn battle…that is nothing. They are being reinforced everywhere. Where are ours to come from, unless they wait & let us grow some.
—Mary Boykin Chesnut, February 16, 1862

To many in the Carolina Lowcountry, Savannah was the sister city to Charleston, but the two were different in several ways. Charleston was a peninsula, with the Atlantic Ocean just beyond its harbor. Savannah was miles upriver from the ocean. Charleston's footprint was somewhat different, as well. Whereas Charleston's early Grand Model had laid the city out in blocks, Savannah was a series of public squares, with blocks arranged around them. In 1861, the squares were crowded with local folks discussing, and even debating, the war, the cotton crop and the threat of Yankee reprisal.

Arriving in Savannah, Lee wasted no time in spreading the alarm and ordering his men to patrol the creeks for any sign of a Federal advance. More heavy guns were moved into the city, adding to those already in place at Fort Jackson.

A bewildered General Sherman wrote again to General Meigs on February 5 about concerns that had hobbled his movements from the beginning:

I fear now, as the season has so far advanced, we shall do little but simply garrison the coast. I am not my own master. My master thus far have been the exigencies created by want of means and facilities for operation in a way desirable to both ourselves and the country at large.

Savannah should have been in our possession by this time, not in the way expected by the anxious public on our arrival here, for of all the visionary and impracticable ideas that could have been invented, nothing could have

Savannah celebrates Georgia's secession. *Courtesy of the Library of Congress.*

equaled that of marching on Savannah on landing here; but by a distinct process, in combination with the navy, either in besieging it by Montgomery, or taking it by the horns by boldly ascending the Savannah River under cover of the gunboats. For the former mode our siege material has never arrived. For the latter mode the opportunity has now unfortunately passed.

Unaware that his Northern counterpart was grinding to a halt, Lee pressed on with the work of preparing the city for a siege. Lee found it necessary to remove certain batteries from sites he determined were overexposed or unnecessary. Guns on Saint Simons Island and Jekyll Island were moved inland. In so doing, Lee observed:

The channel between Saint Simon's and Jekyl's Islands leads into Brunswick harbor…Brunswick is a summer resort for certain planters, and is the terminus of the railroad…there are no inhabitants now in Brunswick, and the planters on the islands have removed their property to the interior; nor is there any population in the vicinity of Brunswick that would seem to warrant jeopardizing the men and guns necessary elsewhere.

Having inspected works around Savannah that were not finished, Lee marveled at the lack of progress and the absolute failure of his officers to make progress in his absence. General Lee wrote to his wife on February 8, and laid the blame for the failed defense works at the feet of lazy laborers:

> *I wrote to you, dear Mary, the day I left Coosawhatchie for this place. I have been here since, endeavoring to push forward the works for the defence of the city, which has lagged terribly & which ought to have been finished. But it is difficult to arouse ourselves from ease & comfort to labour & self denial. Guns are scarce, as well as ammunition & I shall have to break up batteries on the coast to provide, I fear, for this city. Our enemies are endeavouring to work their way through the creeks that traverse the impassable & soft marshes stretching along the interior of the coast & communicating with the sounds & sea, through which the Savannah flows, & thus avoid the entrance of the river commanded by Fort Pulaski.*

Georgia's governor wrote to Lee on February 8, 1862, regretting the necessity of the guns' removal. On February 10, Lee responded from Savannah:

> *No one can regret the apparent necessity of such a measure more than I do, and so great is my repugnance to yield any point of our territory to our enemies, that I have endeavored from the time of my arrival to give strength to the defenses of Brunswick. I find it impossible to obtain guns to secure it as I desire and now everything is required to fortify this city.*

On February 16, Confederate Brigadier General H.W. Mercer sent a message to Captain T.A. Washington, suggesting the following:

> *Before finally evacuating this position, I beg to bring to the consideration of the general the question of burning the town of Brunswick. For the moral effect it would produce upon the enemy, as evidencing our determination to continue the present contest with unconquerable determination and at every sacrifice, and for the other obvious reasons, which you will it needless for me to recite, I would respectfully urge that I be furnished with precise orders to destroy all the buildings that can afford shelter and comfort to the enemy.*

Washington passed the request to General Lee, who took pause at the issue. Mindful of the level to which the Yankees had stooped in blockading Charleston Harbor with the stone fleet, Lee would not rush into a decision to destroy anything unless it was clearly beneficial to the war effort of the

Confederacy. Too easily, a well-intended tactic as suggested by Mercer could be touted by the enemy as propaganda—Rebel raiders, out of control, looting and burning. Lee would at first have nothing to do with it. Instead, he wrote to General Cooper, aid to Secretary Benjamin, on February 18:

> *Brunswick would prove a convenient and healthy position, if occupied by the enemy, affording shelter and comfortable quarters for the troops and hospitals for the sick. It is used as a summer resort, and at this time mostly uninhabited. Should it fall into possession of the enemy, its convenient harbor, salubrious climate and comfortable buildings might tempt him to hold it for the continuance of the year, and rather than it should fall into his hands, I propose to destroy it. Before issuing orders to this effect, I desire that my views be known to the Secretary, so that if not approved by him I may be informed.*

Then, in deference to Governor Brown, Lee wrote the same day:

> *I wish to give directions in reference to the town of Brunswick, provided the enemy attempt to possess…its destruction would deprive the enemy of comfortable quarters…and the hotel serving as a hospital for the sick. As there are other considerations besides those, purely military, involved in this question, I am unwilling to order the destruction of the town without the knowledge and approbation of your excellency.*

Governor Brown gave a hearty response:

> *I have to say that if my own house were in Brunswick I would certainly set fire to it, when driven from it by the enemy, rather than see it used by them as a shelter. We should destroy whatever the military necessities require…private property and private rights must yield to the great public interests now at stake.*

Satisfied that an order of destruction penned by him would not be misconstrued, Lee issued the necessary directives. Eventually, the wharves, the lighthouse and the hotel were burned, leaving the Yankees little to make of Brunswick other than a pallet under the stars.

As Lee struggled to reinforce Savannah, the Confederacy was elsewhere being pushed into a corner. On February 6, Fort Henry in Tennessee fell to an armada of Union ironclads and wooden gunboats under the command of Flag Officer Andrew Foote. Led by the ironclad *Carondolet*, over one hundred shots were fired into the fort, commanded by Brigadier General Lloyd Tilghman, who soon was aboard the *Cincinnati* surrendering to Foote. Foote, in turn, handed him over to Captain Henry Walke, who recalled later entering the Confederate fort after the battle:

> *The first glance over the fort silenced all jubilant expressions of the victorious. On every side lay the lifeless bodies of the victims, in reckless confusion, intermingled with shattered implements of war. Our eyes then met each other's gaze with a sadness, full of meaning, that forbad any attempt to speak, and, in the quietness like that of a graveyard, we walked slowly over the desolate scene.*

On February 8, Roanoke Island was lost to the Federals. Roanoke's three thousand Rebels were under the command of Lee's former nemesis Henry Wise. Thirty-two guns were shared among four batteries, none of which covered the lowest point of the island where Union General Ambrose Burnside and his almost eight thousand men landed.

Though Southern casualties numbered fewer than 100, almost 2,500 were taken prisoner. This victory gave the Union an excellent base from which to control most of the North Carolina coast.

While looking for battlefield trophies on Roanoke, the Union soldiers were disappointed to find only a mixed collection of knives, pistols of all sorts, flintlock rifles, hunting rifles and a few percussion conversions. The Yankees wondered how the Rebels made any kind of stand at all so poorly equipped.

Next to fall was Fort Donelson. General Grant had moved his army overland to combine with Foote's armada. The February 14 assault forced the Confederate commander Brigadier General Simon Buckner to surrender, and that surrender was to be unconditional. General Grant thus showed, early in the second year of the war, what kind of commander he was. Upon hearing of the events, Lee knew that sometime, whether the war lasted another month or another year, he would probably face Grant in battle.

In a letter home, Lee mentioned: "The news from Kentucky and Tennessee is not favorable but we must make up our minds to meet with reverses and overcome them."

Given the string of disasters, the Confederate government immediately made plans to shift forces to meet the Yankee threat in the West. The defense of Florida south of the Appalachicola River was abandoned, and those troops transferred to Tennessee under General Johnston. The transfer order from General Lee caused profound irritation for Florida's Governor Milton, who resented not being given advance notice of the move.

On February 24, 1862, Lee wrote to Milton: "I had previously authorized General Trapier to withdraw the troops & guns…and to apply them to other vital portions of the state."

On March 1, Lee wrote to Trapier, transferring the Twenty-fourth Mississippi Regiment to Murfreesboro, Tennessee:

> *I desire that no delay that you can possibly avoid will take place in forwarding these troops…the recent disasters to our arms in Tennessee, (Fts Henry & Donelson) force the government to withdraw forces employed in the defence of the seaboard.*

By now, Fernandina's Fort Clinch was in Union hands.

As General Lee lost men to reassignment, hundreds of others refused to join the Confederate service for the duration of the war. On February 22, Lee attended church in Savannah, praying for the protection of the city and the preservation of the Confederacy. Fractured as it was, from the top to the bottom, Lee felt the need for some combination of events that would give him more of an opportunity to confront the enemy decisively. In little more than a week, Lee would have his chance.

On March 2, General Lee received a telegram from Davis. It consisted of one sentence, and it conveyed a dire sense of urgency: "If Circumstances will, in your judgement, warrant your leaving, I wish to see you here with the least delay."

This same day, Lee wrote to his daughter Annie: "I hope you are all well, and as happy as you can be in these perilous times in our country. They look dark at present, and it is plain we have not suffered enough, labored enough, repented enough to deserve success."

Lee then laid out clear directives for General Lawton concerning the continued defense of Savannah. Major Long and Captain Ives, both of whom were with Lee during the fire at Charleston, would remain in Savannah. They would continue to mount batteries at Fort Jackson and on St. Augustine Creek. Captain Tattnall would continue to gather any and all available boats for operations in and around Savannah and continue with obstructions in the waterways.

Lee then shared with his officers his view of the enemy's intent: "The probable route of the approach of the enemy…looks now as if he would take the Savannah River…every effort must be made to retard…the further progress of the enemy."

Lee passed through Charleston on March 4 and left for Richmond the very next day. Lawton continued to labor on, while Sherman, forever unhappy with his plight, sat perfectly still. The railroad remained out of the Yankee's reach, and Charleston and Savannah were still held by the Confederacy. The urgency of Davis's note told Lee that now the Federals had their eyes on the biggest prize of all: the Confederate capital!

TRAVELLER JOINS GENERAL LEE

Traveller was raised by Mr. Johnston, near the Blue Sulphur Springs, in Greenbrier County, Va; was of the "Gray Eagle" stock...when the Wise Legion was encamped on Sewell Mountains, opposing the advance of the Federal army under Rosecrans, in the fall of 1861, I was major of the Third Regiment of Infantry in that legion, and my brother, Capt. Joseph M. Broun, was quartermaster...I authorized my brother to purchase a good, serviceable horse of the best Greenbrier stock for our use during the war...he came across the horse above mentioned, and I purchased him for $175 (gold value) in the fall of 1861, of Capt. J.W. Johnston, son of the Mr. Johnston first above mentioned.

When Gen. Lee took command of the Wise Legion and the Floyd Brigade...in the fall of 1861, he first saw this horse, and took a

Traveller joins General Lee. *Courtesy of Washington and Lee University.*

great fancy to it. He called it his colt, and said he would need it before the war was over. Whenever the General saw my brother he had something pleasant to say to him about "my colt" as he designated him.

The Third Regiment was...ordered to the South Carolina coast...upon seeing my brother on this horse near Pocotaligo...Gen. Lee at once recognized the horse...my brother then offered him the horse as a gift, which the General promptly declined, and at the same time remarked: "If you will willingly sell me the horse, I will gladly use it for a week or so, to learn its qualities." Thereupon my brother had the horse sent to Gen. Lee's stable.

In about a month the horse was returned to my brother, with a note from Gen. Lee stating that the animal suited him, but that he could no longer use so valuable a horse in such times unless it were his own...this was in February, 1862...my brother wrote me of Lee's desire to have the horse, and asked me what to do. I replied at once "if he will not keep it then sell it to him at what it cost me." He sold the horse to Gen. Lee for $200 in currency, the $25 having been added by Gen. Lee to the price for the horse in September, 1861, to make up for depreciation in our currency from September to February, 1862.
—Thomas L. Broun, August 10, 1886

CHAPTER 11

General Lee's Army

I see in Richmond the women go in their carriages for the wounded, carry them home and nurse them. One man was too weak to hold his musket. She put it on her shoulder & helped the poor wounded fellow along.
—*Mary Boykin Chesnut, June 3, 1862*

O n March 13, General Order No. 14 came from the Confederate adjutant and inspector general's office to place Lee "at the seat of government under the direction of the President…charged with the conduct of military operations in the armies of the Confederacy."

The Confederate Congress had voted to put a general in the War Department, a vain attempt to temper Davis's direct involvement in the movement of troops in the field. Though Lee was apprehensive about yet another staff assignment, he went right to work with a sense of enthusiasm and energy, both much-needed qualities amongst a staff laboring daily under the strain of Davis's quirks.

While in Richmond, Lee was quartered at the Spotswood Hotel, with an office at Mechanic's Hall. The hotel was right on the Richmond Petersburg Railroad. Richmond was quite a different city than when Lee left. Brigadier General John Winder, the provost marshal, kept order among the troops visiting on leave. There was a provost jail and a prison for Northern troops. Every available space was given over to the care of the wounded.

Behind the scenes at the Confederate capital, President Davis's subordinates were experiencing ongoing difficulties with their leader's demeanor; two secretaries of state had resigned. John Beauchamp Jones was clerk to whoever happened to be the Confederate secretary of war—there would eventually be five. Jones was a writer and journalist, with experience writing on life in the West and the South. Jones's diary gave a frank assessment of the relationship between Lee and his president:

> *General Lee is doing very good service in bringing forward reinforcements from the south against the day of trial, and an awful day awaits us. It is understood that he made fully known to the President his appreciation of the desperate condition of affairs and demanded carte blanche as a condition of his acceptance of the position of commanding general. The President wisely agreed to the terms.*

Writing to his wife, Lee commented:

> *I have been placed on duty here to conduct operations under the direction of the President. It will give me great pleasure to do anything I can to relieve him and serve the country, but I do not see either advantage or pleasure in my duties. But I will not complain, but do my best.*

Lee's duties involved endless correspondence and conferences with visitors who were in the capital to see one official or another. Couriers brought innumerable dispatches from the field, many of an urgent nature requiring immediate attention.

On March 16, General Lee wrote to General Theophilus H. Holmes, commanding Fredericksburg, Virginia. Holmes was a career soldier and had formally been an officer in the North Carolina militia:

> *I very much regret to learn from your letter of the 14ᵗʰ that it is the opinion of yourself & officers, that Fredericksburg is in itself untenable. Can it be maintained by occupying a position on the left bank of the river or in advance of the hills on that side?*
>
> *I request that you will cause an examination of the country to be made, should you not be sufficiently acquainted with it, both in your front and rear, with a view to make the best position the case admits of. I would also suggest that arrangements be made to break up the railroad to Aquia Creek & remove the iron as soon as in your judgment it can be done without detriment to the service. I think it certain the enemy will press his advance on Richmond in every direction. Our troops are coming in spiritedly, & if we can gain time, I trust we shall be able to drive them back.*

Thus began a long series of communications between Lee and his commanders in the field. His choice of words encouraged and suggested, but did not command. Davis was in command, and at times, Lee would invoke the president's name to coax his men along.

On March 17, Lee addressed General Johnston, commanding at Culpeper Court House, Virginia. Lee did not share Holmes's sentiments that Fredericksburg was necessarily the target of a Yankee advance:

> *From what is stated of the condition of the roads, I hardly think an immediate movement against Fredericksburg can be made, nor am I aware of anything that indicates with any degree of certainty what route the enemy will adopt in his march towards Richmond.*

On March 18, Lee corresponded with General John B. Magruder, commanding the Army of the Peninsula in Yorktown, Virginia. Like so many other officers to serve on both sides during the war, Magruder was a West Point graduate, veteran of the Mexican War and, to the delight of many men around the campfires, an amateur songster.

Lee's concern was the ironclad *Monitor*, which was causing a concern because of its perceived invulnerability to shot and shell:

> *Should the* Monitor *appear before your batteries, it has occurred to me that by reserving your fire until she arrives near and discharging by word of command or simultaneously your heavy guns at her turret at the time when her gun was protruded for delivering fire, if the gun was struck it would be disabled, or if the turret was hit by a number of shot it would be deranged or capsized from the center. Wrought-iron shot are being forged with a view to penetrate her armor. Some will be sent you.*

The ongoing dilemma of not getting enough men to muster for the cause was discussed in a letter to General Edward Johnson, commanding at Monterey, Virginia. Johnson had had some success in the Rich Mountain campaign and had been nicknamed "Alleghany" as a result. To Johnson, Lee voiced his concerns about recruiting:

> *I regret to learn that the prospect of calling volunteers to your aid from the country in which you are operating is so unfavorable. It is important that you call out the militia, as authorized by the proclamation of the governor, to fill up your companies of Virginia regiments to 100 each, concerning which you will receive instructions.*

Lee took time to write to his wife on March 22, 1862:

Our enemies are pressing us everywhere & our army is in the fermentation of reorganization. I pray that the great God may aid us & am endeavouring by every means in my power to bring out the troops & hasten them to their destination.

President Davis spoke through Lee in addressing the need to combine forces to meet the Union troop movements. To General Johnston, Lee wrote on March 25:

The president desires to know with what force you can march to reinforce the Army of the Peninsula or Norfolk. Both armies are now threatened by the enemy assembling in great numbers…from the accounts received nothing less than twenty or thirty thousand men with the troops already in position, will be sufficient successfully to oppose them…the object of the President is to prepare you for a movement which now appears imperative, as no troops are available but those of your army to meet the enemy concentrating on the coast.

Lee wrote to General Benjamin Huger in Norfolk, giving precise directives as the Yankee army approached. Huger was a native of Charleston and had been an official observer to the Crimean War. Lee directed that Huger:

Watch vigilantly the movements of the enemy and endeavor to discover his plans…should Richmond be the object of his attack, and his route be by the peninsula, you must throw across James River at a point to reach his front as large a force as can be safely withdrawn from the defense of Norfolk…you must therefore immediately look to all your defences, organizing the troops to hold them, mobilize the remainder to move at a moment's warning, should they not be required to oppose the enemy in the lines around Norfolk.

You will also have to arrange means of transportation, should it be necessary to cross your troops over James River. The infantry it is suggested might be sent to railroad to City Point and ferried over by steamers. Artillery could be crossed lower down, from Carter's Wharf to Grove's Wharf unless the enemy's gunboats prevent it. But as to the best points and means, you must judge, and make such preparations under both contingencies as are necessary.

For the better part of a year, Davis and Johnston had been at odds over Johnston's assertion that his rank in Confederate service did not reflect his experience and rank in the old army. Because communication between the two was fractious, Lee reiterated to General Johnston the president's prerogative in a letter from headquarters on March 28:

> *The President is not at all reluctant to take the responsibility of any movement of the propriety of which he is confident, and it is only designed to ask of you that judgment which your better information enables you more safely to render. He desires you to exercise that judgment and give him the benefit of your views. In the mean time, if doubtful of the course to be pursued, he invites you to a full conference at this place, where the latest intelligence is collected.*

Despite the demands placed upon him at headquarters, Lee could not dismiss personal concerns for his family. With the Federals on the move, he felt it best for his loved ones to move, as well. Lee wrote to his wife on April 4, warning her not to seek refuge at Rooney's plantation home:

> *One of the probable routes to the latter city is up the Pamunkey. Should they select that, their whole army &c. will land at the White House. To be enveloped in it would be extremely annoying and embarrassing, as I believe hundreds would delight in persecuting you all for my & F[itzhugh]'s sake. I do not think their respectable officers would authorize such proceedings, but believe they would not be able to prevent them. I think it better, therefore, that you should all get out of the way. No one can say what place will be perfectly safe or even quiet, but I think a locality within the route of the invading army will be least so.*

With much regret, Lee withdrew even more troops from the lower coast. On April 10, Lee dispatched a telegram to General Pemberton, who now held Lee's previous post. The telegram was one of great urgency: "Beauregard is pressed for troops. Send if possible, [General Daniel S.] Donelson's brigade of two regiments to Corinth. If Mississippi valley lost, Atlantic states will be ruined."

A little more than a week later, Lee wrote to Pemberton in South Carolina, needing more men in Richmond, but having no men or arms to send to the coast:

> *I regret very much to be obliged to reduce the force in your department, & would rather increase if possible. But from present appearances it will be necessary to collect additional troops to oppose the advance of the enemy, who has now reached the Rappahannock, & may move upon Richmond*

from that direction as well as from the coast, where he is assembling large bodies of troops...I have no arms to send from here but pikes, which you might place in the hands of the men at the batteries, & give their guns to troops in the field, by a proper distribution of guns & pikes in this way, the troops that are now unarmed might become effective.

Lee's plan for General Jackson and his forces in the valley was to hold up any attempt by Federal General Nathaniel P. Banks to join with the other Union forces moving to Richmond. Lee knew that once these armies combined, the Confederacy would have great difficulty holding its lines. To Jackson, Lee wrote on April 21:

I have no doubt an attempt will be made to occupy Fredericksburg and use it as a base of operations against Richmond. If you can use Genl Ewell's division in an attack on Genl [N.P.] Banks and to drive him back, it will prove a great relief to the pressure on Fredericksburg...I do not know whether your column alone will be able to hold Banks in check and prevent his advance up the valley, but if it will, and there is no immediate need for Genl Ewell's command with yours, I would suggest the propriety of its being held in readiness to reinforce General Field...Genl Field has abandoned Fredericksburg, burned the bridges over the Rappahannock and retired fourteen miles south of the town.

As the Yankee threat drew closer, Lee again pondered his family's welfare. In his letter to them, he spoke of a dire situation. He wrote to Mrs. Lee on April 22:

There is another consideration, for it is always well to look at the worst phase of a subject, suppose the army is driven south of James River & you are encompassed in the enemy's lines. How are you to live? The Confederate money would be valueless & the Virginia money perhaps not very current. But there is the difficulty & it has been in view of these sad reverses, which God in his mercy forbid may ever happen, that I recommend a more distant move to Carolina or even Georgia. This is for your own consideration & not for public discussion which would only be mischievous.

On April 25, Lee wrote to Jackson from Richmond:

I have hoped in the present divided condition of the enemy's forces that a successful blow may be dealt them by rapid combination of our troops, before they can strengthen themselves…the blow wherever struck must, to be successful, be sudden and heavy…the troops used must be efficient and light. I cannot pretend at this distance to direct operations depending on circumstances unknown to me and requiring the exercise of discretion and judgment as to time and execution, but submit these suggestions for your consideration.

General Lee gave further encouragement to the efforts of General Richard Ewell in the valley. Lee wrote on the same day:

I think the enemy is establishing a strong force at that point, with a view perhaps of making a diversion or a real attack against Richmond. It has occurred to me as probable that for this purpose he has stripped his line between the Rappahannock Bridge and Manassas; if not, it must be so weakened that I hope a blow from the combined forces of yourself and General [T.J.] Jackson can destroy him.

Lee's support over just a period of weeks was well received by Jackson. Though at the time Lee's role was unknown to most, his dispatches to Jackson had shown how just the right coordination of troops could keep the Yankees bottled up.

Jackson enjoyed success unrivaled by any other Confederate commander, beating the enemy at McDowell, Front Royal, Port Republic and Winchester. Over four thousand Union prisoners were taken, and millions of dollars in supplies were now under Rebel guard. The effort to combine these units with McClellan's forces, for a united attack against Richmond, had now fallen apart.

On May 8, Lee wrote to Ewell:

From present indications it is thought that the column under Genl Banks will attempt to form a junction with that opposite Fredericksburg under Genl McDowell. If you ascertain this to be the fact, an opportunity might be presented for interceding Banks' march & striking him a blow while en route for Fredericksburg.

General Lee knew little short of a miracle could prevent the Federals from merging. Surprisingly, the combined drive on Richmond was halted by none other than President Lincoln, who, at 4:00 p.m. on May 24, sent General McClellan the following telegram:

In consequence of General Banks' critical position I have been compelled to suspend General Mcdowell's movements to join you. The enemy is making a desperate push upon Harper's Ferry, and we are trying to throw General Fremont's force and part of General Mcdowell's in their rear.

Without the anticipated reinforcements, McClellan began to encircle Richmond, about seven miles from the center. On the twenty-seventh of May, Jones reported: "General Lee is still strengthening the army. Every day additional regiments are coming. We are now so strong that no one fears the result when the great battle takes place."

Jones continued on the twenty-ninth: "More troops marching into the city and General Lee has them sent out in such a manner and at such times as to elude the observation of even the spies."

With Johnston now preparing an offensive, his second in command, General Gustav W. Smith, whose health Johnston described as "precarious," did what he could to assist. Smith had previously served as an instructor of engineering at West Point and later as street commissioner in New York. It was Johnston's responsibility to formulate an attack strategy that would save Richmond.

This same day, Lee had sent his secretary, Colonel A.L. Long, out onto the field to inform Johnston that he wished to serve in some capacity in the

General Gustavus Smith.
Author's collection.

coming fight. In the evening, Lee received a welcome from Johnston, just as a violent storm broke, bringing a deluge that caused the Chickahominy to swell to flood stage. All around, the terrain was reduced to muddy bogs.

Johnston and his forces were at Seven Pines, a junction on the Williamsburg Road near a rail depot known as Fair Oaks. Seven Pines was just seven miles east of Richmond. Johnston's plan called for two flanking attacks, with Major General James Longstreet hitting the enemy's center, supported by Major Generals Huger and D.H. Hill. Lee found General Johnston and was about to discuss the proposed strategy, when President Davis rode up. Perhaps to rally his men, or perhaps to get away from Davis, whom he detested, Johnston mounted his horse and rode for the front.

On the thirty-first, an 8:00 a.m. attack did not come off until after 1:00 p.m., in part because Longstreet was delayed in moving his men. Huger asserted that he was delayed crossing a rain-swollen stream. It would be late afternoon before Longstreet advanced. The delay had caused Lee and Davis to ride out toward the sounds of cannon fire. Soon they found themselves carried along in a sweeping Rebel attack that was failing against Yankee artillery.

As day dwindled to dusk, the firing subsided, but neither Davis nor Lee had left the field of battle. The recent downpours reduced the battlefield to a quagmire, with some soldiers waist deep in mud. Davis soon got word that Johnston had overexposed himself to enemy fire and was terribly wounded. A Minié ball had struck Johnston in the shoulder, and a shell fragment pierced his chest. Johnston was carried to the rear and command fell to General Smith.

Davis quizzed Smith on what his plan was for the next day's engagement. The second in command rambled on about not knowing what Longstreet or D.H. Hill had to deal with at first dawn and was unaware of just what Union forces were in his front. When pushed by the president, Smith conceded that he had no plan at all.

Smith's inability infuriated Davis, who may have had a passing thought of taking charge of the offensive right then and there. When first caught in the action that day, he had found himself sending dispatches here and there, trying to get a better picture of the confusion that reigned all around him and General Lee. Prudently, he now sent Lee to meet with Smith, whose health was again deteriorating.

In the evening, Smith was informed by General Stuart that, despite the flawed coordination of troop movements, Longstreet had nevertheless succeeded in pushing the enemy back beyond Seven Pines, well past their second line. General Huger had not engaged at all, and D.H. Hill's division had done most of the fighting. General Johnston's official report would find great fault with Huger, who would, in turn, appeal to President Davis for an investigation.

Regardless of any differences among Longstreet and others, the reality of the battle remained the same. By now, the capital of the Confederacy was just one big hospital. Seven Pines had left almost five thousand men wounded, with almost a thousand dead on the battlefield. Jones recalled in his diary a young soldier from the Carolinas:

> I saw a boy, not more than fifteen years old from South Carolina, with his hand in a sling. He showed me his wound. A ball had entered between the fingers of his left hand and lodged near the wrist, where the flesh was much swollen. He said smiling: "I am going to the hospital just to have the ball cut out and will then return to the battlefield. I can fight with my right hand."

The thirty-first of May came to a close, but the battle outside Richmond was not over. Mr. Jones's account of the day was poignant:

> The battle did not occur at the time specified. General Huger's Division was not at the allotted place of attack…his excuse is that there was a stream to cross…towards sundown it was apparent that the entrenched camp had been taken. At night. The ambulances are coming in with our wounded. They report all the enemy's strong defenses were stormed.

Major Steedman fought at Seven Pines, as well. He recalled the glorious haul of goodies taken from the Union camps:

> The booty was very rich and every man loaded himself with such an assortment as best suited his wants or fancy. Besides clothes of every description, blankets, rubber oil clothes, knapsacks, and the other appurtenances of the soldier, we brought away fine Enfield and Austrian guns, and would have equipped our companies had there been ammunition with the abandoned guns. We obtained also the first coffee which many of us had tasted in months, and found a liberal supply of lemons also in a sutlers' tent, besides hams, whiskey and all kinds of commissary stores in profusion.

Obviously concerned about maintaining his rank and status, Smith sought to mitigate the president's fury by showing he did have some sense of a strategy for the day's engagement. He sent a dispatch to Lee early on the morning of June 1, with details of his planned attack utilizing the forces on his right. There, Major General John B. Magruder commanded several brigades, including Kershaw's Second South Carolina, which had not fought the previous day. To this message, Lee replied:

> *Your movements are judicious and determination to strike the enemy right. Try to ascertain his position and how he can best be hit…you are right in calling upon me for what you want. I wish I could do more. It will be a glorious thing if you can gain a complete victory.* .

On June 1, the Yankees attacked again. Johnston's official report tells the early events of that day:

> *On the morning of June 1st, the enemy attacked the brigade of General Pickett, which was supported by that of General Pryor. The attack was vigorously repelled by these two brigades, the brunt of the action falling on General Pickett. This was the last demonstration made by the enemy. Our troops employed the residue in securing and bearing off the captured artillery, small-arms, and other property, and in the evening quietly returned to their own camps.*

President Davis later rode up to Smith's headquarters and asked for General Lee. According to Smith, the moment was rather awkward:

> *On being told that I had not seen General Lee during the day, the President expressed so much surprise that I asked him if he had any special reason for supposing General Lee would then be there. To this he replied yes, and added that early in the morning he had ordered General Lee to take command of the army at once. This was the first intimation I received of the assignment of General Lee to the Army of Northern Virginia. I answered: In that case he will probably soon be here…General Lee arrived about 2 p.m., and at once took command of the army.*

Davis was still in great need of Lee on his staff in Richmond, but he knew now that the army defending the capital needed a new leader. Nothing about Smith gave the president confidence, and the president's choices were few: Johnston was in bad shape, Albert Sidney Johnston had been killed and Beauregard was serving in the Western Theatre, as far from the president as possible. On the ride back to Richmond the previous evening, Davis handed over command to Lee, with a promise to issue a formal order in the morning.

D. Augustus Dickert, now captain and commander of Company H, Third South Carolina Infantry, described Lee's ascension to command:

> *General Lee took command the next day, June the 1ˢᵗ, 1862. He did not come with any prestige of great victory to recommend him to the troops, but his bold face, manly features, distinguished bearing soon inspired a considerable degree of confidence and esteem, to be soon permanently welded by the glorious victories won from the Chickahominy to the James.*

Early on the morning of June 2, the Confederate forces began their withdrawal, while General Smith, by his own admission, was too ill to remain on the field.

General McClellan's vain attempt to capture the capital of the Confederacy had failed, and the Union had a new Confederate commander to deal with. Lee now had an army of his own. Upon his shoulders rested the fate of the struggling Southern Republic, for which he must ultimately strike a victory.

Back in Richmond, Lee issued General Order No. 22, which, for the first time, formalized in writing the new name of the army:

> *In pursuance of the orders of the President, General R.E. Lee assumes command of the armies of Eastern Virginia and North Carolina…every man has resolved to maintain the ancient fame of the Army of Northern Virginia, and the reputation of its general and to conquer or die in the approaching contest.*

By the end of June 1862, the Seven Days Battles would be hard fought and won, and the Confederacy would have new faith in its army and its new leader. General Robert E. Lee would emerge as a masterful tactician for whom Federal generals would pause to give due consideration before facing him in battle. He had persevered and had been victorious. Lee would urge perseverance among his troops to the very end, until their hunger and sheer exhaustion near Appomattox would cause him to selflessly seek an end to their suffering. This compassion would cause Lee to be remembered by his men to the end of their days as a true "soldier's general."

The legacy of General Robert E. Lee continues today, an inspiration to anyone who has faced insurmountable odds and eventually prevailed. It is a legacy that will live in perpetuity.

Bibliography

Anderson, Nancy Scott, and Dwight Anderson. *The Generals: Ulysses S. Grant & Robert E. Lee.* New York: Wings Books, 1987.

Ballard, Michael B. *Pemberton, A Biography.* Jackson: University Press of Mississippi, 1991.

Bennett, C.A. "Roswell Sabin Ripley: 'Charleston's Gallant Defender.'" *South Carolina Historical Society Magazine* 105 (1994).

Black, Robert C., III. *Railroads of the Confederacy.* Wilmington, NC: Broadfoot Publishing Co., 1987.

Bradlee, Francis B.C. *A Forgotten Chapter in Our Naval History. A Sketch of the Career of Duncan Nathaniel Ingraham.* Salem, MA: The Essex Institute, 1923. Pamphlet.

Brock, R.A., ed. *General Robert Edward Lee.* Atlanta: H.C. Hudgins Co., 1897.

Burton, H.W. *The History of Norfolk Virginia.* Norfolk: Norfolk Virginia Job Print, 1877.

"Captain James Boatwright." *Confederate Veteran* 8 (1900).

Carbone, John S. *The Civil War in Coastal North Carolina.* Raleigh, NC: Division of Archives and History, North Carolina Department of Cultural Resources, 2001.

Chichester, C.E., Mrs. *A Lady's Experience Inside the Forts in Charleston Harbor.* South Carolina Historical Society, 1895. Pamphlet.

Cooke, John E. "A Life Of General Robert E. Lee." *Edinburgh Review* (April 1873). Pamphlet.

Coulter, E. Merton. *The Confederate States of America, 1861–1865.* Baton Rouge: Lousiana State University Press, 1950.

Craven, Avery, ed. *To Markie: The Letters of Robert E. Lee to Martha Custis Williams*. Cambridge, MA: Harvard University Press, 1933.

"David L. Walker." *Confederate Veteran* 16 (1908).

Davis, William C. *Battle at Bull Run: A History of the First Major Campaign of the Civil War*. Garden City, NJ: Doubleday, 1977.

Dickert, D. Augustus. *The History of Kershaw's Brigade*. Dayton, OH: Morningside Bookshop, 1973.

Dowdy, Clifford. *Lee*. Boston: Little, Brown & Co., 1965.

Dowdy, Clifford, ed., and Louis H. Manarin, assoc. ed. *The Wartime Papers of R.E. Lee*. Boston: Little Brown & Co., 1961.

Evans, Gen. Clement A., ed. *Confederate Military History*. Extended edition. 17 vols. Wilmington, NC: Broadfoot Publishing Co., 1987.

Fishwick, Marshall W. *Lee after the War*. New York: Dodd Mead & Co., 1963.

Flood, Charles Bracelin. *Lee: The Last Years*. Boston: Houghton Mifflin & Co., 1981.

Foote, Shelby. *The Civil War, a Narrative*. New York: Random House, 1958–74.

Freeman, Douglas Southall. *R.E. Lee: A Biography*. New York: C. Scribners & Sons, 1934–35.

"General Lee on Sewell Mountain." *Southern Bivouac* 1 (1883).

"General Robert E. Lee's War-Horse." *Confederate Veteran* 6 (1898).

Grant, Ulysses S. *Memoirs and Selected Letters*. New York: Viking Press, 1980.

Hagood, Johnson. *Memoirs of the War of Secession*. Columbia, SC: The State Company, 1910.

Heyward, DuBose, and Herbert R. Sass. *Fort Sumter*. New York: Farrar & Rinehart Inc., 1938.

Horn, Stanley F., ed. *The Robert E. Lee Reader*. New York: Grosset & Dunlap, 1949.

Jones, John B. *A Rebel War Clerk's Diary*. New York: Sagamore Press, 1958.

Jones, Rev. William J. *Life and Letters of Robert E. Lee, Soldier and Man*. New York: The Neal Publishing Co., 1906.

Letter. New York, March 9, 1862. No. 43/2113. South Carolina Historical Society.

"Letters From Mr. Calvin Conner To Miss Ellen O'Leary, His Sweetheart." *Recollections and Reminiscences* 2 (1994).

Long, A.L. "Lee's West Virginia Campaign." In *The Annals of the War*. Philadelphia: The Times Publishing Co., 1879.

Long, E.B., and Barbara Long. *The Civil War Day By Day*. New York: Da Capo Press, 1971.

"Major Julius J. Wagener." *Confederate Veteran* 25 (1917).

Manigault, Gabriel. *Memoirs*. South Carolina Historical Society.

Marszalek, John F., ed. *The Diary of Miss Emma Holmes, 1861–1866*. Baton Rouge: Louisiana State University Press, 1979.

McCabe, James D. *Life & Campaigns of General Robert E. Lee*. Atlanta: National Publishing Co., 1866.

Mercury, November 1861–March 1862.

"My Experience as a Soldier in the Confederate Army." *Recollections and Reminiscences* 5 (1994).

Nevins, Allan. *The War for the Union*. 4 vols. New York: Scribner & Sons, 1959–71.

Nolan, Alan T. *Lee Considered: General Robert E. Lee and Civil War History*. Chapel Hill: University of North Carolina Press, 1991.

"Pea Ridge Volunteers." *Recollections and Reminiscences* 1 (1994).

"Personal Experiences of a Veteran—W.J. Courtney." *Recollections and Reminiscences* 1 (1991).

Pryor, Elizabeth Brown. *Reading the Man*. New York: Viking Penguin, 2007.

"Reverend Samuel Davies Boggs, D.D." *Confederate Veteran* 22 (1914).

Rowland, Lawrence S., Alexander Moore and George C. Rogers Jr. *The History of Beaufort County*. Columbia: University of South Carolina Press, 1996.

Smith, Gustavus W. *The Battle of Seven Pines*. Dayton, OH: Morningside Bookshop, 1974.

South Carolina Ordnance Bureau. Ordnance Bureau Records, 1860–61.

Stern, Phillip Van Doren. *Robert E. Lee: The Man and the Soldier*. New York: McGraw-Hilll, 1963.

Stevens, Hazard. *The Life of Isaac Ingalls Stevens*. Boston: Houghton Mifflin & Co., 1900.

Taylor, Walter H. *Four Years with General Lee*. New York: D. Appleton & Co., 1878.

"Tennesseans in the Mountain Campaign, 1861." *Confederate Veteran* 22 (1914).

"To Coosawhatchie in December, 1861." *South Carolina Historical Society Magazine* 53 (1952).

Turner, Charles W. *Captain Greenlee Davis, C.S.A. Diary & Letters, 1861–1865*. Verona, VA.: McClure Press, 1975.

United States War Department. *The War of the Rebellion: Official Records*. Series 1, vol. 6. Washington, DC: Government Printing Office, 1899.

Walke, Henry. *Naval Scenes & Reminiscences of the Civil War in the United States*. New York: F.R. Reed & Co., 1877.

Winston, Robert W. *Robert E. Lee: A Biography*. New York: Grosset & Dunlap Publishers, 1934.

Wise, Stephen D. *Lifeline of the Confederacy: Blockade Running During the Civil War*. Columbia: University of South Carolina Press, 1988.

Woodward, Glenn, ed. *Mary Chesnut's Civil War*. New Haven: Yale University Press, 1981.

Woodworth, Steven E. *Davis & Lee at War*. Lawrence: University Press of Kansas, 1995.

Young, James C. *Marse Robert: Knight of the Confederacy*. New York: Rae D. Henkle Inc. Publishers, 1929.